PROXIMITY

TO

DEATH

Yankee Stepfather:
General O. O. Howard and the Freedmen

Grant: A Biography

Frederick Douglass

Sapelo's People:
A Long Walk into Freedom

Proximity to Death

PROXIMITY
TO
DEATH

William S. McFeely

W. W. NORTON & COMPANY

NEW YORK / LONDON

Copyright © 2000 by William S. McFeely

All rights reserved
Printed in the United States of America

First published as a Norton paperback 2001

For information about permission to reproduce selections from this book,
write to Permissions, W. W. Norton & Company, Inc.
500 Fifth Avenue, New York, NY 10110

The text of this book is composed in Bodoni Book
with the display set in Bodoni Bold
Composition by Platinum Manuscript Services
Manufacturing by Quebecor Printing, Fairfield Inc.
Book design by JAM Design

Library of Congress Cataloging-in-Publication Data

McFeely, William S.
Proximity to death / William S. McFeely
p.   cm.
Includes bibliographical references and index
ISBN 0-393-04819-5
1. Trials (murder)—Georgia. 2. Capital punishment—Georgia—History.
I. Title.
KF221.M8M39   1999
345.758'0773—dc21   99-31293
CIP

ISBN 0-393-32104-5 pbk.

W. W. Norton & Company, Inc., 500 Fifth Avenue, New York, N.Y. 10110
www.wwnorton.com

W. W. Norton & Company Ltd., 10 Coptic Street, London WC1A 1PU

1 2 3 4 5 6 7 8 9 0

for Mary and Maggie
and
for Stephen Lucas

. . . any soldier will tell you, if he tells the truth,
that proximity to death brings with it a corresponding
proximity to life.

—Tim O'Brien
The Things They Carried

CONTENTS

PREFACE

ALL BOOKS TAKE on a life of their own as they are being written, but this one simply jumped out at me—alive from the start. I responded to a telephone call asking me, as a historian, to offer factual "expert" testimony in a pretrial hearing. I turned up to do so and found myself face to face with a convicted murderer whose own life was in his lawyer's hands. As I drove away from the courthouse, this book was already beginning to take shape in my mind.

I have never had any trouble knowing where I stood with relation to the value of the death penalty, and others who oppose it will have little difficulty placing themselves in relation to this story of lawyers, clients, and jurors. Neither will those who unequivocally and, it seems, irrevocably favor the use of executions as punishment for lethal crimes. But it is just possible that it will be a different matter with readers who lean toward capital punishment out of concern for a victim, or as being appropriate for mass murderers and terrorists whose bombs kill scores of innocent people.

From the first day in court, "murderer" ceased to be simply a category of criminal for me; here was a man convicted of murder who was, vividly, a very particular person. As the book carried me along, I came to know four such people. I sat in the same room with Carzell Moore, Kenny Smith, Tony Amadeo, and William Brooks. I came to know, too, their lawyers and, after one defendant's trial, the jurors. The book was not written to persuade. But it does deal with an issue that is very much in the public discourse. It may be that simply the telling of the story of a Stephen Bright pleading a case, a Johnny Hubbard judging it, will contribute to that discourse.

ACKNOWLEDGMENTS

SO MANY PEOPLE helped in the writing of this book that I feel certain that I will forget to thank someone. If so, my sincere apologies.

At the beginning, two colleagues at the University of Georgia helped get me ready to be "expert." Jon Houghton generously turned over his thorough notes on the relationship of the Confederate battle flag to the Georgia state flag. John Inscoe gave me a historian's version of moot court as I tried out my analysis of lynching.

Librarians at the University of Georgia—in particular Charles L. Barber—at Harvard University, and the Wellfleet Public Library were helpful. Two old friends and superb legal scholars, Milner Ball at the Georgia School of Law and Aviam Soifer at the Boston College Law School, opened resources for legal scholarship to me. Two students at those law schools—now fine young lawyers—provided indispensable help to this neophyte at legal research. Gerald Ells, at Georgia, not only was diligent in finding research materials, but was insistent that the story be told. Nicholas Stellakis at Boston College was a model

1 2 / ACKNOWLEDGMENTS

of the careful, imaginative researcher. His meticulous attention to detail, along with his patience with my thousand and one queries, made him a colleague rather than an assistant.

Jennifer Sargintsen of the Georgia Department of Corrections arranged permission with Warden Wendy Thompson to visit William Brooks when all earlier attempts to gain it failed. Laverne McLaughlin at the Albany State College gave me a room to work in the day of my visit to the Jimmy Autry State Prison. Oliver Keller taught me much about Georgia prisons. The staff of All Souls Unitarian Universalist Church in Washington confirmed facts about their building. In Columbus, Bill Winn was immensely generous in sharing not only his remarkable recreation of the T. Z. Cotton story but also his insight into racial matters. Similarly, Gary Parker instructed me in the ways of criminal justice in Muscogee County. Phyliss Barrow enlightened me on Madison, and her husband, Judge James Barrow, was a great help as I acquainted myself with the structure of Georgia courts and the issues raised there. Charlie Knox introduced me to McDuffie County, and, better, to Blind Willie McTell.

Everyone at 83 Poplar Street was so helpful that I do not want to embarrass them with recitals of virtues, but I do want to thank Robin Toone and Mary Sinclair. Not directly involved in the death penalty cases, Robin seemed an almost-neutral person to check out some of my readings of those cases; again and again, Mary's searches turned up crucial details. In New York, George Kendall took time out from a calendar as crowded as those in Atlanta for long, enlightening conversations, and also for twice reading drafts of the manuscript. Another superb defense lawyer working with indigent clients, Henriette Hoffman, read early and late drafts of the book. I'm certain the final product does not reach these lawyers' high legal standards, but they undoubtedly kept me from some of my most egregious errors.

Jennifer McFeely offered an invaluable insight into the complexity of the feelings of victims' families. James Goodman not only goaded me on but gave the whole manuscript the benefit of his fine writer's eye. Eliza McFeely, too, added her acute historian's observations. And, while we're on the family, Mary Drake McFeely read section after section with her remarkable editorial eye; Drake McFeely said keep it short.

Donald Lamm once again proved what a superb editor he is. Twice he read and made line-by-line suggestions to strengthen the prose. The proof of his remarkable professionalism lies in the fact that the subject of this book is one far from his own interests. Sarah Stewart, Nancy Palmquist, and the whole of the Norton team have been exceedingly helpful; Ann Adelman was an excellent copy editor. Georges Borchardt, my agent, made valuable suggestions. Sebastian Junger alerted me to David Von Drehle's *Among the Lowest of the Dead*. And it was my good friend Philip Hamburger who gave the title the right slant.

I profited from talks in the hall with my colleagues at the University of Georgia—Bryant Simon was expert on pharmacology and Mark Cooney on homicide—and from a discussion of the work at a seminar arranged by Robert Allison at Suffork University. The colloquium at the W. E. B. Du Bois Institute at Harvard was stimulating, helpful, and encouraging. I am deeply grateful for Henry Louis Gates, Jr.'s question that day, for his friendship, and for providing me with a scholarly home at the Institute.

I hope their story, impossible to tell without their remarkable candor, indicates how immensely grateful I am to the two prisoners, Tony B. Amadeo and William Anthony Brooks. Similarly, the jurors I talked to were remarkably forthcoming. It is not hard to find condescending comments about those ordinary people who compose juries in the United States, but I would like someone to show me citizens—at any level—who took their responsibilities more seriously and selflessly than did the twelve residents of Morgan County, Georgia. In this assessment, I very much include those who disagree with me about the death penalty and said so. I will never forget the conversations with many of these quiet, frank people who have so much that is admirable in common.

PROXIMITY
TO
DEATH

1

A Georgia Courthouse

WHEN I DRIVE from Athens to Sparta, I know I am in Georgia. The road takes you through open fields. Only one sharecropper shack remains, light peering through between the four piles of bricks on which it stands. Cotton, mechanically maintained now, is regaining its place in competition with the beef cattle endlessly grazing on gently sloping hillsides. Coming into Sparta, the county courthouse commands attention.

Falsely promising to block the way, the monumental building rises straight ahead. Tall and wide, with white wooden lace falling over rich red brick as its high windows point toward the bright white of the cupola crown, this is the law's palace. Georgia's grandiloquent courthouses are her architectural glory. Creaking majesty may be a lot for a worn-down town to carry, but whether, as here in Sparta, in splendid raiment or where prosperity has forced the law to don drab modern garb, the courthouse reigns in each of the state's 159 counties.

There is nothing ridiculous about the courthouse's power. The feet of many citizens have worn the treads of the stairs as, for decades, they have climbed to the upstairs courtroom to watch neighbors learn their fate at the hands of justice.

Courtroom drama here in Georgia, as everywhere, is plentiful. Sometimes it slips close to comedy. A dog gets into a chicken yard and kills most of the fowls. The owner is found guilty of his dog's crime. It shouldn't be too hard for the jury to assess damages. The only problem is that these were not run-of-the-mill 89-cents-a-pound chickens that were consumed; they were valuable fighting cocks, a value not diminished by the illegality of cock fighting in Georgia. Nothing, it seems, is simple.

The stakes are higher, in some eyes at least, if, another day in that courtroom, the dead body is that of a person brutally murdered and what is before a jury of peers is the decision to put to death the person guilty of that murder. Under the law of Georgia, acceptable to the nation's Supreme Court, these citizens of the state must decide whether to kill the killer.

There are few subjects grittier than the death penalty. Its curious appeal lies, in part, in its very grimness. For proponents, their eyes on the moment of terrible murder and the bereft family of the person killed, there is the Judgment Day finality of the act of execution. For opponents, most of whom reject the validity of any killing, even as punishment, there is the compelling suspense of the sentencing, and later, the wait for a judge's final stay, a governor's last-minute clemency—followed by the ineffable, helpless sadness when neither comes and they watch the doomed man's last hours, choreographed to the beat of the clock moving to the moment of his extinction. In either instance, deep emotion is at work.

On another day, when I drive over to Jackson, not far across the state from Sparta, confronting me is a very different structure. Amid stretches of an incongruously manicured park of sloping green surrounding a pond stands the low-lying, gleaming prison in which live the men—in Georgia they are still all men—awaiting death. For those unable—or even unwilling—to get help staving off execution, the wait will be less long than for others with competent lawyers. And yet the wait for most is considerable. In Georgia, the average time between conviction and execution is in excess of eight years; many have been on death row for more than twenty years. Even a man who wanted to die had to wait out appeals others filed for him. For those with lawyers at work, this wait, kept afloat by hope, stretches out over the years while the maddeningly baffling business of appeals and retrials works its way through the system.

Some of the men on death row at Jackson are among the clients of a group of lawyers forty-five miles north in Atlanta at the Southern Center for Human Rights. A phone call to the center is answered, simply: "Law Offices." There is no question but that law is practiced here. Stephen B. Bright is first among equals of these less than a dozen lawyers whose work is keeping their clients alive. Unlike those who zealously work to end the death penalty by trying to bring moral pressure at every point in the society where a decision to end the death penalty might be made, Bright and his colleagues fight to keep individuals from experiencing it. The law they so skillfully practice often, in other hands, works violence. These lawyers are determined to keep each of their clients from the ultimate expression of violence, the state killing its own people.

However complex the law as the work progresses, the identity of the center's clients is never lost in some theoretical attack on what might prove to be their fate. In the lawyers' daily conversations with each other and with their clients, each prisoner is, by name, Kenny or William, Carzell or Tony.

There are many, including the present chief justice of the United States, who, approving of the death penalty, hope these lawyers will not succeed. The Congress, with the justices' blessing, has already shortened the condemned persons' wait—and their chances of survival—by limiting the ability to appeal to the federal courts. All across the land there are cries for more executions. Governors who have held out against the death penalty are defeated; politicians, former prosecutors prominent among them, climb to elected office on its popular coattails. The task of ending the death penalty, thought accomplished by an earlier Supreme Court in 1972, has seemed almost hopeless since 1976, when executions could be resumed. Until revived, the death penalty had not been exacted since 1967. In 1997, the states killed seventy-four people; thirty-seven in Texas alone.

In 1995, Congress voted to end funding for the twenty resource centers which provided counsel for death-sentenced inmates in the later stages of court review where lawyers are not furnished by the various states. Thwarting efforts to save convicts' lives, rather than economy, was the motive in many lawmakers' minds as they eliminated the federal program. Lawyers at the centers also provided advice to volunteer lawyers who often had no experience with capital cases. With the end of funding for the resource centers, the burden on the privately funded agencies grew heavier.

It was in 1995, also, that Congress, in the aftershock of the Oklahoma City bombing, launched an assault on the writ of habeas corpus, the law's avenue of appeal to the highest court of the realm.* In the United States, the "great writ"—once sacred to citizens of a democracy, and particularly to its lawyers—has been seen as available for appeal from a sentence both in a state court and in the federal courts. In over roughly 40 percent of the cases appealed, federal district courts and the courts of appeal have found constitutional errors in the state courts' proceedings and have reversed death penalty convictions.

Despite the constitutional vagaries the lower federal courts so often found in state court decisions, the present Supreme Court, over the last decade, has been determined to establish the primacy of the states and their review processes. In so doing, the highest court of the realm is turning back a movement by its predecessor courts toward a reading of the Fourteenth Amendment that holds that even in such local matters as law enforcement the country's populace are citizens of a nation as well as a state and protected by federal law.

*The Antiterrorism and Effective Death Penalty Act of 1996, limiting appeals, was signed April 24, 1996. In 1994, Congress had provided for fifty new federal capital crimes.

The rub is that those citizens invoking protection are some-times unsavory criminals. Twentieth-century appellants are no longer, as they once were, corporations, which, in the nineteenth century coopted the Fourteenth Amendment and persuaded the Supreme Court to regard them as people. Many are convicts seeking redress; and with the rise of violent crime in the 1970s, powerful people sought to prevent their finding it. But not by making a frontal assault on the Fourteenth Amendment. The strategy rather was to restrict the seeking of remedy to the state courts, and to limit the time and grounds for death penalty appeals to federal courts. To end, in Senator Orrin Hatch's oft-repeated phrase, "these frivolous appeals," would be to speed the awful vengeance of the law and assert dominion over a threatening criminal class composed largely of the poor.

HOW CAN THOSE of us for whom both the concept and the real-ity of the death penalty are repugnant be expected to keep the faith? A clue comes from an unlikely source. In "The Black Cottage," a poem by Robert Frost that I have read many times over the years, a minister and the narrator, out for a walk in the woods long after the Civil War, come upon an abandoned house. The woman who lived there, the clergyman muses, stood for a cause now almost forgotten: the freeing of the slaves. And she held to her obsolete belief "That all men are created free and equal." Those two causes, both beyond saving the Union, were what "she thought . . . the Civil War was for."

Now, half a century later, "These doorsteps seldom have a visitor. / The warping boards pull out their own nails . . ." The lonely house seems to the clergyman a lifeless reminder of actions and words that no longer matter. He muses on the mean-ing—or rather, the lack of meaning—that the house symbolizes. Then he suddenly notices that

> There are bees in this wall." He struck the clapboards,
> Fierce heads looked out; small bodies pivoted.
> We rose to go. Sunset blazed on the windows.[1]

For the woman living in the house, the antislavery cause must once have seemed close to hopeless. The 1850s witnessed enforcement of the Fugitive Slave Act, talk of reopening the African slave trade, and the *Dred Scott* decision asserting that African Americans had no rights that white citizens need observe. Yet she lived to see slavery end, and the Reconstruction amendments that were supposed to ensure freedom and equality made the law of the land.

When the minister and the narrator came across her empty house, the nation seemed to have abandoned its post–Civil War commitment to equality for the people freed by that war. In the South, where most African Americans lived, the repression of Jim Crow laws and terrifying lynchings were accompanied by disenfranchisement. And yet, at the very time Frost wrote "The Black Cottage" (it was published in 1914), a small band of Americans had begun the twentieth century's long, unfinished march toward racial justice. The old woman's ideas do sting with life.

In our time, a small, determined group of people, whom she would have recognized as spiritual kin, refuse to give up the struggle to end what they see as a fundamental wrong in our society. Indeed, the anti–death penalty effort is not far apart from the nineteenth century's antislavery movement. Descendants of slaves have suffered a disproportionate number of imposed deaths. But race, decidedly a factor in the death penalty debate, does not alone define the issue. The death penalty in fact cuts even more deeply into the whole fabric of the society. Many, perhaps the majority of Americans presently regard capital punishment as necessary to the ordered weave of society. For others, it is a moral snag that must be undone. The most dedicated opponents of the death penalty work against seemingly hopeless odds, but still hope to see light blaze on their window.

THIS IS AN account of some of them, lawyers and clients who combat the death penalty in Georgia's courthouses. It is the story too of jurors who have to decide if a person is to die or live. It is not a treatise on the legal intricacies of death penalty law, nor is it an account of those with the fortitude to befriend inmates during their long wait and stand by them in the harrowing hours on the day they die.[2] There is here neither sociological analysis nor a comprehensive history of the death penalty in the United States.[3]

Instead, this is an account of a historian who suddenly found himself pulled out of history and into the reality of the law taking a person's life. Right in front of me, as a result of twenty minutes on the stand as a witness in a death penalty case, appeared what seemed to me a strand of the hatred that has done, and continues to do, great damage in the land.

I know something of the nation's history—of the history of its violences—but one day in a Georgia courtroom carried me beyond a recording of the past toward a small responsibility for the present. And so this book is simply a story of a few people living in one corner of the country who carry a large responsibility. The dry boards of a Georgia courthouse creak into life when one person—a lawyer—in defiance of a society that no longer cares, goes about the tough, unpopular work of trying to keep us from killing his client, the person sitting next to him.

2

The Grand Dragon

T HE LAST OF an early morning fog lifts from the courthouse square in McDonough, a town in central Georgia.
Cars and pickups shuffle neatly into and out of roads
meeting at its four corners. On one corner, the classic bank
building is now a pawnshop; on another is the breakfast and
lunch café. Across the common, thick with trees and bordered
with late summer flowers, the white-steepled pile of brick and
curved granite of the 1897 Henry County Courthouse, like its
even more ornate cousin in Sparta, stands tall.

Up the worn stone steps and out of the nineteenth century, I
climb the interior stairs and enter a neatly modernized small
courtroom. Only its pressed tin ceiling belongs to the past. A
history teacher never before with such an assignment, I am
innocent of every particular of the coming event save one, its
central issue. The previous Monday, September 25, 1995, the
telephone rang in my University of Georgia office in Athens.
When the caller identified himself—"This is Stephen Bright"—
it took only two mental clicks for the name to register.

I had been told by a lawyer friend in New York that Stephen

Bright was one of the best of the lawyers fighting the death penalty, but had not met him. Would I, Bright asks now, be an expert witness at a hearing on motions that he will present before the judge who will conduct the sentencing trial in the case of Carzell Moore? Needed is someone familiar, first, with the history of the Georgia state flag, two thirds of which bears the stars and bars of the battle flag of the Confederacy. The Confederate battle flag, waved at Ku Klux Klan rallies, was added to the state flag in 1956, the days of massive resistance to integration. Bright will contend that a black person is not equally protected by the Fourteenth Amendment to the Constitution in a room in which, approvingly, a racist emblem is displayed.

Secondly, Bright says he needs someone familiar with violence in the South. I gently remind him that this is a fairly big topic. Somewhat vaguely, he brings up lynching and a link to the death penalty. With the mention of lynching, I tell him the person he wants is Fitzhugh Brundage, author of *Lynching in the New South*.[1] I haven't finished the citation when Bright cuts in: "He's up in Canada." The man knows the literature, and even the whereabouts of its perpetrators. And I'm not off the hook. Turning to the flag, I ask Bright if he wouldn't prefer to have it discussed in softer southern tones rather than my Manhattan rasp? "No," he replies. Out of excuses, and curious, I say, "Yes, I will be in McDonough at the courthouse on Thursday at nine."

TAKING A SEAT now at the end of a row in the spectators' section, I try to read the topography of the unfamiliar furnishings in the almost empty courtroom. I recognize the judge's bench high in the corner with the American and Georgia flags drooping on either side, but am not sure of much else. Across, at what I take to be the lawyers' table, a big-chested black man is going through papers pulled from thickly stuffed accordion files. His fashionably shaved head makes his age hard to guess—perhaps thirty-five. He's wearing an up-to-the-minute dark suit with high-peaked lapels over a pinpoint blue shirt and silver and navy patterned tie. Things can't be all bad in Georgia, I think, if we have African American lawyers like this one taking capital cases. Through his thin-rimmed round spectacles, he peruses the documents with precision, pausing only to greet quietly others joining him at the table.

It is just after nine o'clock. As the room fills, the judge, balding and dapper in a camel's-hair jacket, enters from his chambers and quickly, formally identifies those present at the bar. Glancing hurriedly around, I try to find the defendant—he can't be the young man in the row in front of me; the prisoner would not be sitting with the spectators. It's an hour into the testimony before I can convince myself that the well-set-up man at the lawyers' table is Carzell Moore, a convicted kidnapper, rapist, and murderer.*

One of those seated, or rather perched, at the crowded defendant's table is a tall white man with a strange sheath of dull copper hair who never seems to alight for long. Almost with a rush of air, he has come into the courtroom carrying energy with him. Toying with glasses, constantly on and off, he appears to be everywhere in the room at once. Not a large man, even a little narrow in the shoulders, he seems almost to fill the space. This has to be Stephen Bright.

In this courtroom he is in action, but not in command. Bright has an adversary, the Flint Circuit district attorney, Tommy K. Floyd. Deliberately languid, slow to rise to a dignified height, his handsomely graying wavy hair perfectly combed, Floyd sits most of the day with his long legs sprawled under his table. But there is a look almost of contempt on his face as he peers over half glasses at the defense lawyer. Perhaps it is all simply courtroom posture, but I sense more.

It is not that Bright and Floyd are two able lawyers capable of playing interchangeable roles in a legal game, as their professor in law school might once have had them do. Quite the

---

*Only later did I learn that Moore was wearing a stun belt under his suit jacket. If at any time it seemed warranted, the deputy monitoring the device could have sent an electric shock to Moore's kidney area that would have incapacitated him.

opposite. They stand as exemplars of two fundamentally differ-ent philosophical positions on the death penalty. Bright and Floyd guard gates—of different cities.

Carzell Moore has been convicted for an act so terrible that neither guardian would lightly allow this man the freedom of his city's streets. One, to sustain the city, would use the law's authority to banish from life a being no longer within his concept of human; the other would claim that no person is ever wholly outside the city's wall. Though Moore has raped and murdered—has sacked his own city—he is, to Stephen Bright, still of its people. For the authorities of that city, for its citizens, to match his act of killing with a killing, to deny even him life, is for the city to lose its very civility.

In December 1976, Teresa Allen, a young white woman work-ing as a clerk in a Cochran convenience store, was abducted by two black men, Roosevelt Green and Carzell Moore. They drove her forty miles north, then raped and shot her. Both men were apprehended and jailed, pending trial which was to be held in Forsyth, the seat of the county in which her death took place. Green escaped from jail and Moore, in his absence, was tried, convicted, and sentenced to death. Green was traced to South Carolina when he made a telephone call to a mutual acquain-tance inquiring about Moore. Brought back to Forsyth, Green was tried, and, after further litigation, executed. Meanwhile, the Center had taken Moore's case; errors in the penalty phase of his trial were established and he was granted a new sentencing trial.

In this courtroom in a town distant from Forsyth where Carzell Moore was tried and convicted, Judge Joseph B. Newton from Waycross, even farther down state, is conducting a hearing prior to the new jury trial that he will convene to determine whether Carzell Moore will live out the rest of his life in prison or die. The judge has entered this case, which has been moved to this courthouse, as a result of the long appeals process that has successfully challenged the fairness of the orig-inal sentencing.

To be heard and contended for are a cluster of arguments by Bright and his colleagues maintaining that Moore has been denied—and is in danger of again being denied—equal protection of the law under the Fourteenth Amendment. At the same time, Bright will be building—with a freshness that almost suggests this is the first time he has done so—an argument that the death penalty is inherently wrong. This double strategy is at work throughout the day. Any conceivable maneuver allowed by law that might buy Moore's life more time is brought forth in tandem with the underlying principle that the state has no license to take that life.

At their table, facing the judge, is Moore's legal team. Alongside Bright sits Palmer Singleton. With his rumpled suit and unruly thatch of black-brown hair, he could stand in for a professor. But absent-minded, no; when it's his turn to go after a witness, the voice is as gravelly as Bright's is clear; he is firm and decisive. (Neither has an accent that spells region.) At Singleton's right is a woman as visible on any street as he would be inconspicuous. I had seen her earlier crossing one in McDonough, striding purposefully on long legs toward the courthouse, briefcase in hand. Her well-shaped head was shaved into a Mohawk, with the surviving hair corn-rolled and pigtailed down the back of her neck. Although, later, Bright would pointedly refer to her as "African American," that touch of the warpath together with the corporately correct tailored jacket and high heels made a mockery of any single label for Althea Buafo. She has joined Bright's team for the case.

In a chair pulled up to the far corner of the table is a still younger woman, Tanya Greene, proudly introduced to the court by Bright as the center's first Blackmun Fellow from the Harvard Law School. The mention of the name Harry Blackmun, the Supreme Court justice who turned against the death penalty, is all that is needed to make unequivocally clear that there will be no diffidence about proclaiming exactly where this band of lawyers stands on the death penalty. Justice Blackmun (who died in March 1999) in 1994 left the ranks of those on the

Supreme Court protecting the death penalty and reinvigorated opponents across the country with his announcement that he would no longer "tinker" with the "machinery of death."[2]

Years earlier, a conservative attorney general in Pennsylvania had, one day, come upon the room in which stood that state's lethal machine, an electric chair. He took one long look at the chair and the containers into which witnesses to an execution could vomit, and came close to throwing up himself. Fred Speaker hadn't, before that moment, taken in just what a capital case, a death penalty came down to. He bided his time. But after the election of his successor, minutes before yielding office, he dispatched a written order to the warden of the prison housing the long-unused electric chair to dismantle it. Accompanying the letter was a formal legal opinion declaring the death penalty to be cruel and unusual punishment under the Eighth Amendment. The warden may have been happy to carry out the order; not a few other wardens required to orchestrate executions have spoken of how painful the task is. The demolished electric chair was later replaced by another, only to be replaced, in its turn, by a gurney with the insidious intravenous needle close at hand.[3]

Carzell Moore, the man on whom the machinery is likely to work—Georgia still has its electric chair—sits not facing the judge but at right angles to him. With his back to the wall, Moore is in plain sight of the four deputy sheriffs—one black, the others white—who, in shifts of two, stand across the room at either end of the empty jury box constantly watching the prisoner. Occasionally, one of the deputies, his big gut drooping over the railing, swaps knowing smiles with the other at some lawyer's familiar antic. The two remind you of any relaxed, nice guys drinking iced tea you might sit next to at a lunch counter. At a break, two of the deputies escort Moore to the bathroom. The three return seemingly sharing a joke.

There are no jokes in the formal proceedings, no down-home joshing. The subject is death, but the discourse is of flags and statistics. In Georgia, we have had a glorious ruckus over the state flag. I suspect that there are a good many loyal citizens of sister states who, if pressed, would have trouble recalling much of anything about the cloth fluttering over official buildings. Not here. Little can inflame an assemblyman or assemblywoman like a call to defend the flag—or to defy it. One need look no further than present-day Georgia for evidence that rippling cloth can have potency. Either it stands for our southern way of life and no one may rip it down, or it stands for oppression, like a swastika, and must be banished.

ON FEBRUARY 8, 1956, with a governor braying that no Negro child would ever enter a white child's school, the all-white General Assembly of Georgia passed a resolution of interposition. That great exponent of states' rights, John C. Calhoun, was back at his post protecting southern civilization from the law of the land. The legislators sought to nullify not only the Fourteenth Amendment but also the Thirteenth, with its two related purposes, the ending of African slavery and the prevention of its replacement with any substitute. For the Georgia legislature to toy with the idea of a return to slavery in order to counter the 1954 Brown versus the Board of Education decision requiring an end to segregation in schools was to send a transparent message to Georgia's citizens of African descent.

To overcome any ambiguity, the assembly, the next day, February 9, passed legislation replacing the old Confederate horizontal bars that, since 1879, had covered two thirds of the state flag with the Confederate battle flag, its unmistakable St. Andrew's Cross riding on a field of defiant red. Unmistakable, too, is the flag's significance. Anywhere in the fifty states, its presence on a pickup truck's bumper says no to black Americans.

Georgia's governor, Zell Miller, knew that in 1993, when in a remarkable state of the state address to the legislature he called for the removal from the state banner of the Confederate battle flag, which, he contended, "challenges the very existence of the United States of America. And ... exhibits pride in the enslave-

ment of many of our ancestors."⁴ He was jeered. After months of
public controversy, faced with the certainty of the defeat of his
initiative to rid Georgia of the battle flag, he had his proposal
withdrawn. Miller lost that battle. And, for fighting it, many
expected him to be defeated for reelection. He was not.

Now, in September 1995, Stephen Bright puts on the stand
the first of three dignified, gray-haired citizens of Georgia:
Tyrone Brooks, veteran of the civil rights movement and now a
representative in the state legislature. "And you are African-
American, just for the record?" inquires Bright. "I think I am
African-American, for sure," Brooks replies, and tells of his
objection to what the flag signifies.⁵ Then C. T. Vivian testifies.
A former minister, Vivian achieved fame for the film footage
showing him being beaten by a sheriff's club during the famous
civil rights protest at Selma, Alabama. He, in turn, is followed
by Joseph Beasley, who left a Georgia county with no high
school for black students to study in Ohio and is now southern
regional director for Jesse Jackson's National Rainbow
Coalition.

All three, having been over this ground a good many times,
make it clear that the battle flag—whether displayed unalloyed
at Klan rallies and in the windows of pickups, or incorporated
into the state flag that hangs in restaurants, in schools, and in
courtrooms—is not, for them, a sign of welcome. Rather, it is a
statement of implacable racism. Attorneys Bright and Buafo are
attempting to show that the flag standing at Judge Newton's side
sends a signal not only to a black defendant but also to a jury
that all Georgians are not equal under this flag, which symbolizes the state's lawful authority. It will be my job to back up their
contention with some history.

One's name called out loudly and clearly in a courtroom has
a compelling ring. I step through the low gate and take the oath.
Bright stands directly in front of me, my eyes to his a taut line
of telepathy. He begins by making me sound as expert as possible, extracting credentials; books published, prizes won, titles
held—including, pointedly, that I recently held a professorship

named for Senator Richard B. Russell, the still-revered staunch defender of segregation. (Many think this stand may have cost a powerful senator the presidency.)

To the faithful in the room—perhaps the judge is one—I can't, with that imprimatur, be all bad. Or, if irony has its way, maybe I can. Perhaps I will prove to the loyalists just how upside down everything has become: the state university has committed a desecration.

I find myself giving a schoolteacher's recital of the history of the Confederate battle flag (as distinct from the official flag of the Confederate States of America). The brilliant red silk, emblazoned only with the blue and white St. Andrew's Cross across its middle, was run into battle, accompanied by the rebel yell, in the terrible, noble days of the War of Northern Aggression. It flew, as well, after the war when Klansmen rallied and rode to surround a Negro cabin. The whole black county knew the terror, I report, when one black person was dragged out of the cabin and killed.

Mention of the Klan alerts Bright. His intensity seems almost to pull from me a recital of the use of racial violence by the Klan and other, less organized groups to intimidate the freed people and defeat the political gains they had made during Reconstruction. Moving further along in the nineteenth century, I distinguish the Klan's work from "another form of violence, which is . . . in a certain sense, more terrible and germane to matters before us today . . . lynching."[6]

As I mention 460 such occurrences in Georgia, of which in 411 cases the victim was black, District Attorney Floyd objects: "How can an illegal act of lynching . . . be relevant to these proceedings. . . ? I object on the grounds of relevancy."[7] This is what Bright is waiting for. He intends, he tells the judge, to inquire as to "the relationship between lynching and the death penalty," and, to that end, cites as the time of linkage the 1930s, when the "pro[functory] death penalty trial" took the place of lynching. By this he means a trial where a judge, with the town's reputation at stake, moves to prevent the removal of a prisoner from a jail for an extralegal hanging. He lets it be known that the trial will be swift; the jury dependable; and his sentence, "hung by the neck until dead," forthcoming.

Bright does not explicitly—not yet—equate the citizens' cry for a death by lynch mobs in the 1890s, or would-be lynchers in the 1930s, to today's instruction, "Burn 'im," heard when a murder suspect is booked. Nor has he yet implied that the prosecutor, though using more temperate language, is essentially uttering the same cry with a swift call for the death penalty after a man is accused of murder.

Bright turns back now to the 1890s, lynching's worst decade, to get me to underscore the linkage of death by the rope to death by electric current. Meekly, but perhaps wisely—I do not want the tale to be so strident as to blur the analogy—I tell of the death in 1899 of Sam Hose, leaving out much gruesome detail. To facilitate attendance at that spectacle, advertisements announcing plans for the man's killing ran in the Atlanta papers for excursion trains to Newnan, Georgia, where the killing was to take place. When Bright asks what the "mood" would have been at such an event, I reply, tepidly: "They were celebrations."[8]

AS I WALK down the courthouse steps in search of some lunch, a pleasant-looking man who had been sitting in the spectators' section directs me to the restaurant on the far corner of the square, and goes off in his own direction. In the café, with its home cooking and the inevitable iced tea, I'm invited to join three other spectators—an outspoken local woman in clerical garb, and a quiet couple who, I finally piece together, run a hostel in Jackson where they assist families of men on death row who come, often from long distances, to visit. The almost homey daily life of attending death suddenly becomes immediate as the two talk matter-of-factly about their work.

Back in the courtroom, the legal team goes about its work in much the same spirit. Mary Eastland takes the stand on the question of whether racism infects the choice of jurors. A lean, intense woman, bemused by being asked by Palmer Singleton, whose office is next door to hers, "Where do you work?" and wondering if that fact will make her testimony seem biased, answers, "I work at the law offices." "Located where?" "In Atlanta." When Singleton is still unable to get the formality of employment established, the judge intervenes and Eastland says, wrestling with the awkwardly obvious answer, "Well, Mr. Bright's, Mr. Singleton's."[9]

It takes many questions for Singleton to elicit from his remarkably diligent, intelligent investigator just how thorough has been her study of the racial component of the juries in the Flint Judicial District. With exquisite caution, she explains how she has gone into every imaginable public record in order to identify the race of those who have been seated or dismissed during the selection of juries in criminal cases in the judicial district in which Moore was tried.

It is hard to imagine where this exchange is going. The answer comes in the testimony of the next witness, Michael Radelet. A sociologist at the University of Florida—the court reporter records him as an "academic socialist"—Radelet has done extensive quantitative research on the role of race in death sentences. He gives an analysis of Eastland's data demonstrating that, when the person indicted was black, prosecutors sought a jury as white as possible. The point is that to do so is to defy the Supreme Court ruling that race cannot be the sole criterion for dismissing a potential juror.[10]

Radelet also presents an analysis which shows that prosecutors in Georgia asked for the death penalty far more frequently when the victim was white and the defendant black than when the situation was reversed or when both were of the same race. We are in the realm of the chi square analysis. (It's "c-h-i s-q-u-a-r-e," for the benefit of all of us in the courtroom.)[11] I am by no means the only one fogging over. But efforts to make Radelet look the bewildering scholar fail. Radelet clearly has firm statistical data; its relevance to this case will be the issue.

In his cross examination, District Attorney Floyd presses

Radelet on the accuracy of his study. In one exchange, they reach the question of the motivation of prosecutors and Floyd states, "he is a racist . . . if he seeks the death penalty?" To Radelet's reply, he mutters audibly, "so we're all racists." Radelet shoots back that he had said no such thing: "I don't think I have used at all the term racist, and I don't think I have called you or anybody in your office a racist." With tempers flaring, Judge Newton orders the expunging of hostile remarks from the record.[12] Decorum, so unctuously exercised, is restored.

THE MAP OF Carzell Moore's case is unfolding. The basic, underlying topography—as wide as the nation itself—is that the death penalty is wrong. Meanwhile, every river and every tributary has been explored in search of a route that will keep one particular person alive. Since the region is the South—though any other would qualify as well—and Moore is a black man, there is a likelihood that racial prejudice played a role somewhere along his route to death row. Proponents of the death penalty contend that race is no longer on the map. Bright and Singleton and Buafo follow every bend in the river to show that race still infects the area; that, specifically, it lies right here in the Flint Judicial District of central Georgia.

Moore's lawyers want to show that the electrocution of a black man is still an occasion for celebration on some Georgia nights. The next three witnesses will be asked to describe the scene outside the Jackson prison the night that Roosevelt Green was executed. (Green, in a separate trial, had been convicted of the murder of Teresa Allen, along with Carzell Moore.)

Wendell Ramage is a pleasant-looking white man dressed neatly in a khaki shirt and pants. His employer? "The Monroe Academy, Incorporated, private school." Everyone in the room knows how to read this language. Ramage's is a segregated private school, one of the hundreds that sprang up in the 1950s and 1960s in defiance of the Supreme Court order to desegregate the public schools. To drive home the point, Bright asks: "Do you have any African-American students?" "No," is the answer.[13]

Getting down to the case in hand, the lawyer asks, "Before you worked at the Monroe Academy, where did you work?" "Monroe County Reporter," where, jack-of-all-trades, he was a reporter covering Roosevelt Green's trial. And, Bright continues, "Did you," in that capacity, "have occasion to attend the execution of Roosevelt Green? . . . Did you, in fact, watch the execution?" "Yes." But Bright does not require that Ramage match Susan Sarandon witnessing the death of Sean Penn in *Dead Man Walking*; he asks instead: "Did you also cover events around the execution?" District Attorney Floyd objects as Bright moves to get the reporter to tell of the gatherings that night outside the Georgia Diagnostic and Classification Center. (The Jackson facility was designed to receive recently convicted felons in order to determine to which prison they were to be sent. After a riot at the Reidsville prison and the escape of prisoners, the center became the home of the electric chair.) Bright responds to the objection by saying that "We'll show" that a "celebration of the execution" is "historically related" to similar behavior at other episodes in the history of racial violence.[14]

Judge Newton overrules the district attorney's objection. Then Ramage describes how "the whole front area [just outside the prison buildings, but within the grounds] had been divided into sections which were filled—one section was filled with press; there was one section that was filled with Ku Klux Klan members; there was a section that was filled with people against the death penalty. I think that there were others, but I don't remember specifically. But what I remember is just a large number of people who were there, all in groups with a cause."[15]

Of one group, Bright asks: "How were they dressed? In robes? The traditional robe of the Ku Klux Klan?" "Yes." "Did they have any signs?" "Yes." "Do you recall what they said?" "I think most of the signs were jingles that said something like, 'Now he's going to burn, now he's going to fry, now he's going to shake, now he's going to die,' that kind of thing. And I'm sure that's not a specific one, but that's the idea. I remember the 'fry' and 'die' and 'shake.' " "And would you describe the mood among that group of people?" "Angry, hostile, and eventually celebrative."[16]

As he has all day, District Attorney Floyd sits impassively at his table, flanked by two upbeat young assistant district attorneys, a man and a woman. Neither of Floyd's assistants spoke to the court during the long day; the woman twisted at her ponytail and dangled a black suede pump from her toes. Cross-examining, Floyd asks (and scores): "Did you see any Confederate Battle flags out there?" "If I did, I don't remember them."[17]

Alfred I. Dube takes the stand. The smiling man who directed me to the restaurant is a civil servant at the Robins Air Force Base, and remembers that word of the grisly death of the young Allen woman "spread all over Cochran and middle Georgia." His heart "went out to the family" and he recalls raising money for a scholarship fund to be awarded at the high school that Teresa Allen attended. I am wondering where this testimony is going when Bright asks Dube if he was on the grounds of the Diagnostic Center the night of Green's execution and learns that he was. "And did you take anyone with you?" "I took my family." "And who would that have been?" "My son, my daughter, and [my then] wife." "And how old was your son at the time?" "He was about 13." "And how old was your daughter?" "She was about 11." Asked what occurred out there on the prison grounds when he heard that the execution had taken place, Dube replies, "I do remember there was some celebrating, you know." "Describe that to us." "When they brought the hearse out, I remember the crowd jumping up and down and celebrating."[18]

The next witness is a tall, rangy white man comfortably wearing blue work clothes. He leans back almost cockily in the witness chair; Stephens, with a "ph," not a "v," he tells Judge Newton when formally asked his name: "Edward Stephens. I've been a master electrician since '78. I've been doing electrical work since I was old enough to hand my father light bulbs, I guess."[19]

"How long have you lived in Georgia?" Bright asks. "All my life." "Have you ever been involved in an organization called the Ku Klux Klan?" "Yes, sir, I have." "Hold any positions in that organization?" "Yes, sir, I have." "What positions have you held?" "I've held everything from a basic klansman, all the way to head of the State of Georgia as the Grand Dragon."[20]

"My duties and responsibilities were to try to educate the public as to what the Ku Klux Klan is about. . . . Keep the people peaceably assembled at any kind of gathering we had. I can say that any of the gatherings that we did have, that we didn't have any violence." "During your tenure?" "Yes, sir. I was regularly and heavily observed by the Georgia Bureau of Investigation and was never observed doing anything illegal." Asked about the position of the Klan with regard to race, he tells of his opposition to having children "force-bused" to school and his belief that "if a man is qualified to do a job, give him the job, whether he be black, white, red, or yellow. . . . And as I told your investigator the other day, the basics that I believe in are the same basics that black people believe in. They're proud of their race, like I am of mine."[21] The legal profession lost a star when Edward Stephens chose electricity.

"Do you recall going to the grounds of the Georgia Diagnostic and Classification Center on the evening that Roosevelt Green was executed?" asks Bright. "I don't remember . . . that particular case standing out over and above the other seven or eight executions that I've went down there in support of the death penalty on, it doesn't stand out for any reason except for my beliefs in the death penalty itself." "Do you recall the reaction of . . . your fellow Klan members when the word came that Roosevelt Green had been executed, or when the hearse passed with the body?" "I don't remember that exact one, but I'm sure it's just like as in a couple of white people that were executed down there, it was the same reaction."[22]

"And what was that?"

"Joyful relief that it's another burden off the taxpayer's back."

"And how . . ." Bright begins.

"Just like," Stephens continues, "I mean for every equal there's an opposite; for every sob, there's a happiness."

"And how is the happiness expressed? I mean, you're there watching . . ."

"The same as the mourning and the sorrow is expressed, in the opposite way."

"What do you mean?"

"Well, where they stand around and hold candles and cry because a person has just been executed. But they don't think anything of the victims. We rejoice that the person that has created the crime, that has taken a person's life and extinguished it like a cigarette butt has been put to rest, and hopefully sent to where he's supposed to be, no matter what color he is."

"No matter what color?"

"Yes, sir."[23]

AT THE CLOSE of the day, Bright entered a swarm of new motions, each likely to be rejected by Judge Newton, each a possible basis for appeal. Meanwhile, Carzell Moore would wait—for another day in court, for six months, even a year away, when twelve other Georgians will decide whether he will go on living in jail, or die. The sentencing trial was to be moved to Thomson, in eastern Georgia's McDuffie County.

Here in Henry County, as the opposing lawyers and the judge cleaned up the tedious business of mislabeled exhibits, Bright was asked if he had anything more to add: "Your honor . . . I would like the record to reflect that the District Attorney and both of his assistants are white. . . ." As he continued, noting that the clerk of the court, her assistant, the sheriff, four of the five deputy sheriffs, were white, Judge Newton interrupted, countering with the fact that Bright and Singleton "are white, as is Ms. ——" The name was not out of the judge's mouth before Bright cut in to correct his identification of the light-skinned Tanya Greene: "Ms. Green[e] is African American, Your honor." "Okay, Ms. Green[e], excuse me . . ." retorts Judge Newton, half-conceding his lost point (and making mockery of all such designations), let it be noted for the record that she and Ms. Buafo "are of African American descent." Bright, unfazed, kept on with the match: "Of course, the Defendant, Mr. Carzell Moore, is of African descent."[24]

I DRIVE NORTH toward my Georgia home. A brazen red and orange *Gone With the Wind* sunset blares over my left shoulder, throwing golden light under precisely spaced pecan trees. Cattle graze on darkening green slopes. I race away from a day so filled with action, with life—all hinging on a man's death—that I cannot make sense of it. But know I have to.

As a historian, I deal with events safely in the past. However passionately I may care about whatever it is I am trying to explain, I know its outcome, know what happened next. What am I doing letting a present-day story, whose ending I do not know, whirl so savagely in my head? It is not simply that I've had a glimpse into the world of the courtroom; rather, I hear the old nineteenth-century issues of race and inhumanity that I've written about before reverberating from today's courtroom walls.

Driving along, I can't silence those sounds with admonitions that I should get back to the nineteenth century. The 1897 Henry County Courthouse no doubt holds secrets of its own time that I might well pursue; but today, the events in a room in that building have pressed into my head a quandary I know I cannot leave behind.

3

Athens

HE CAR ROLLS through the open countryside, my mind
running ahead of the speed limit trying to catch up with
the subject. What makes the carrying out of a death
penalty so chilling a method of killing? Is it that the men who
work down at the prison in Jackson, going about the banal business of bringing a man to the electric chair, are the counterparts
of those nice-guy deputy sheriffs back in the courtroom? Is it the
emotional distance from the room in Jackson, Georgia, where
that chair sits to the august courtroom in Washington, D.C.,
where sit justices of the Supreme Court who sanction, but do not
see, the death? Does the watching or imagining of the hour-by-
hour, minute-by-minute march to the calibrated climax of electric or intravenous death slyly awaken a contemporary prurience
akin to the arousal of those who once thronged to watch the jerk-
ing death of a man dangling from a gallows? Is it the coupling of
technological efficiency with calculated legality?*

---

*A person seated at a remote computer dispatching a missile to murder a street-
ful of people is a chilling killer too, but if we are to accept a distinction between
peacetime and wartime behavior, the death penalty retains its icy singularity.

In the Supreme Court, the day he finally looked the death penalty squarely in the face, Justice Harry Blackmun was facing a case in which the principle that a death sentence must be imposed according to a rigid standard of equality collided with one which held that judges and juries should have discretion, even perhaps some moral flexibility, in imposing so grave a fate. How could those unreconcilables be made to reconcile? They couldn't. Blackmun had had enough of adjusting valves and levers. Announcing his renunciation of the death penalty, the justice said he would no longer "tinker" with the "machinery of death."[1]

But if Blackmun, who had done more than his share of under-the-hood tinkering, was now through with it, his fellow justices were not. Justice Antonin Scalia, in an opinion in the same case that one observer considered surprising and "openly dismissive of another justice's expressed moral anguish,"[2] forthrightly advocated retribution as a proper motivation for the death penalty. And it was Scalia, not Blackmun, who was listening to the overwhelming enthusiasm of a majority of the citizenry for the death penalty. One of the great rallying cries of the 1990s has been the call for the enactment of laws enlarging the number of crimes subject to execution, coupled with virulent demands that the penalty be carried out.

The loudest cries, other than those following such traumatic events as the Oklahoma City bombing of 1995 or a series of torture-murders, come when a convicted murderer is paroled and then commits another murder. This might seem a convincing argument for the death penalty. But studies of recidivism do not point to frequent repeated murders. Of the 558 inmates who had their death sentences commuted as a result of the Supreme Court cessation of the practice in 1972, seven have subsequently committed murders—six while in prison and one when on parole. Seven too many. But it is interesting to note that in Florida alone, three of those whose sentences were commuted were found to have been innocent of the crimes for which they would have been killed. A Michigan study reports that of the four hundred murderers paroled between 1938 and 1972, none had murdered again.[3]

Such studies have not quieted the demand for use of the death penalty in the United States, which runs counter to the modern history of the death penalty elsewhere in the world. The death penalty has been abolished or is in disuse in all the Western European countries and in most of those in the former Eastern European bloc of nations, including Russia. In another two dozen countries, capital punishment laws have not been used for a decade. In Israel, only Adolph Eichmann's death has broken its founding policy of no capital punishment. South Africa, where calls for vengeance might well have been expected in reaction to the widespread legal and extralegal executions of the apartheid era, has discarded state killing as vindictive and inhumane. The quaint sentiment, "forgiveness," is spoken of; it would be rare indeed to hear anyone in power in this country use such a word for a criminal at present.

Why has the United States, with its claim to moral leadership of the world, gone in precisely the opposite direction? Why are we Americans so enamored of the death penalty? Shouldn't it have gone the way of witch trials and slavery? Concepts of civilization called for the banishment of these institutions on the grounds that they were inhumane. In our vigorous use of the death penalty we are in company with Iran, Iraq, the United Arab Emirates, and Yemen. And yet, didn't we, a quarter of a century ago, think the death penalty gone for good?

In a disconnected way, all of this is coursing through my head as, out my left window, the late summer evening sun is blazing through pecan groves. How can there be such light at the end of a day that has introduced me to so dark a subject? How can I have come away with a sense of life being so richly lived in a courtroom where death is the subject?

The vitality I sense in the lawyers trying to keep a murderer alive is the Janus face of an American culture that nurtures a call for his death. In the seventeenth century and on through the eighteenth, public hangings in the colonies were held by many people, including clerics who took the events as texts for grim admonitions, to be salutary warnings to the populace of the wages of sin.

There were others, informed by Enlightenment thinking, who thought that perfecting a civil society required that executing criminals for a great variety of crimes should cease. Thomas Jefferson drafted a bill in Virginia that ended the death penalty for crimes other than murder or treason. As was often the case when it came to societal wrongs such as slavery, it was the Quakers who first sought to end the death penalty altogether. Benjamin Rush, not a Quaker, but a Pennsylvania physician deeply imbued with enlightened secular principles of the new American republic, declared: "Capital punishments are the natural offspring of monarchical governments." A government of the people had no need for them: "An execution in a republic is like a human sacrifice in religion."[4]

Such thinking did not prevail. Orthodox Christians on the one hand and rifle-toting frontiersmen on the other endorsed the death penalty. Where the gentility of the nineteenth century prevailed, a sense of decorum, married to a need for order, dictated that deviants be sequestered in asylums and prisons, and that the gallows be moved out of sight of crowds. Some by this change hoped to quell popular support for the death penalty. From the eighteenth century onward, reformers like Rush have sought ardently and even optimistically to rid the land of capital punishment.

During the 1830s and 1840s, an era of civilizing reform, opposition to the death penalty was one of many efforts undertaken to perfect the society; the antislavery movement, penal reform, humane treatment of the mentally ill, and the temperance movement were others. In 1846, the state of Michigan became the first governing entity in the world to abolish the death penalty. One scholar contends that the anti-capital punishment campaign came close to achieving its goal nationwide and only failed to do so because of the brutalization of society by the Civil War. The killing of American by American on the battlefield, as well as the execution of deserters back in camp, acts deemed to be in a good cause, seemed in a hardened post-bellum world commensurate with a civilian death penalty.[5]

Following the Civil War, as outlaw terrorism was employed to reassert white supremacy in the South, legal executions were given an official imprimatur. State governments removed the authority for hanging from local jurisdictions. Beginning with Vermont in 1864, forty-two states, over the next century, strengthened their authority by centralizing the place of execution and making its exercise conform to standards. This did curb the excesses of local hanging judges responding to local demands for vengeance; but making the death penalty state business also made it a more respectable practice. Those still repelled by executions, state-sanctioned or not, kept up the effort to end them. Later in the century, clergy preaching the social gospel and their parishioners imbued with a more benevolent sense of Christianity joined the crusade.

The reform movement of the early twentieth century was a secular expression of a belief that the society could be perfected. For some, this meant that a well-ordered nation required the death penalty; many others were convinced that a more perfect society had no need of the uncivilized practice of killing its transgressors.

Advocates of the death penalty had their own concept of civilization. They welcomed the invention of the electric chair as a quick means of disposing of a transgressor that was less painful than the hangman's rope. Opponents saw death by a massive flash of electricity as a return to death on the pyre. Defenders of technology knew better. To prove that the electric chair did its job, and did it quickly, Thomas Edison, the reigning expert on things electric, traveled out to the freak shows on Coney Island and electrocuted an elephant.[6]

Not reassured, opponents not merely of the electric chair but of the death penalty in any form went to work. Characteristic of reform movements at the time, the arenas chosen for action were the legislatures of the several states. Between 1907 and 1917, nine states, all of them west of the original thirteen, abolished or sharply limited the death penalty. In others, the opposition to capital punishment was strong even when it did not prevail. And where the law allowed executions, fewer were sought.

This momentum toward reform did not survive World War I. There was a coarsening of public opinion toward longtime citizens of German descent and, just after the war, toward immigrants thought to be in sympathy with Soviet communism. In that climate, five of the nine states that had ceased executions had, by 1920, reinstated capital punishment; two others did so in the 1930s. North Dakota remained free of the death penalty, save in the case of a new murder by a convicted murderer, and in Minnesota there were no exceptions to the ban. But elsewhere, executions increased in number. As mob lynching almost ceased in the 1930s, the number of executions rose: the average per decade from 1880 to 1929 was 1,153; for the entire 1930s decade, the number was 1,676.[7]

The pattern of violence expressed by an increase in executions following earlier wars was broken by World War II. Executions per decade declined from 1,284 in the 1940s to 715 in the 1950s; the figure fell dramatically just prior to the cessation of executions in 1972. The last execution before that year took place in 1967.[8] This rejection of killing seemed to many Americans to be in keeping with the revelations of the horrors of the Holocaust; with the civil rights movement's attempt to end racial injustice sanctioned by law and enforced by acts of violence; and with the repugnance at the killing of native villagers during the nation's war in Vietnam.

In 1972, the Supreme Court acted in the case of William Henry Furman, a mildly mentally deficient condemned black Georgian, who, trying to enter a house, shot at the door and killed the householder on the other side. A Stanford University law professor, Anthony Amsterdam, argued the case with particular brilliance, and five justices, a majority, voted to spare Furman and end the death penalty. All nine justices wrote opinions. Justice William O. Douglas looked at the fact that Furman

was black, saw decisions to execute as "pregnant with discrimination," and in an essay on Anglo-American jurisprudence
held that the evolutionary march of ever more civilizing laws led
to the ending of the death penalty.[9]

With both passion and eloquence, Justice William Brennan
held that "the calculated killing of a human being by the State
involves, by its very nature, a denial of the executed person's
humanity." He closed with seeming finality: "under the Cruel
and Unusual Punishments Clause [the Eighth Amendment to
the Constitution] death stands condemned as fatally offensive to
human dignity. The punishment of death is therefore 'cruel and
unusual' and the States may no longer inflict it."[10]

The lone African American justice, Thurgood Marshall, presented an exhaustive history of the practice. Justice Potter
Stewart saw cruel and unusual punishment in the case before
him, but did not reach the view that the Eighth Amendment
made all executions constitutionally invalid. The capriciousness
of the use of death was enough for him to concur: "These sentences are cruel and unusual in the same way that being struck
by lightning is cruel and unusual."[11]

The fifth of the majority of justices, Byron White, however,
left a foot in the door for the reentry of the death penalty. He
found "the penalty not to be cruel and unusual punishment in
the constitutional sense because it was thought justified by the
social ends it was deemed to serve."[12] For him the error was the
absence of any "meaningful basis" for distinguishing the few
sentenced to death from those who were not.

State legislators were not slow to see that new laws might sweep
away White's objection. He was, in fact, not far distant from the
four dissenters to the Furman majority who, each writing his own
opinion, indicated that if such new laws were enacted, they might
well be allowed to stand. All held that the Court had no right over-
ruling state legislatures, death penalty laws because of personal
revulsion to the practice. Chief Justice Warren Burger said that if
he were a legislator, he would vote against the death penalty, but
as a judge he must respect a contrary law.

Justice Harry Blackmun dissented on similar grounds, but gave a hint of his future stand, noting that capital punishment "is antagonistic to any sense of 'reverence for life.' " He concluded: "Although personally I may rejoice at the Court's result . . . I fear the Court has overstepped."[13] Justice Lewis Powell was sure it had. He would not have been sorry if the various legislatures had abolished the death penalty, but said that it would be "a basic lack of faith and confidence in the democratic process" for the Supreme Court to defy the will of the majority.[14] Justice William Rehnquist—later, as chief justice, to become the death penalty's strongest defender—simply held it was "a penalty that our Nation's legislators have thought necessary since our country was founded."[15]

William Furman's death sentence does not appear to have been a necessity. Orderly in prison, he was paroled in 1984, and today is a construction worker in Macon.[16] Reformers, elated by the Furman decision, chose to be deaf to the dissents and to White's reservations. They cheered and two liberal state supreme courts acted. To forestall any efforts by the legislature to restore capital punishment, judges in California and New Jersey declared it in violation of their states' constitutions. Surely, the next move would be for the Supreme Court to finish the job and find it a violation of the constitutional prohibition of cruel and unusual punishment. And, so went the hope, this humane step would then be embraced by the citizenry nationwide.

Rather than the dawn of the final day of capital punishment, the announcement of the Furman decision gave rise to energetic legislative action to restore it. The eagerness was particularly apparent in the South, where legislators, still largely white, fought in the late 1970s an effective rearguard action to reassert some local dominion over their black fellow citizens. During the 1960s, this supremacy had been eroded by the surprisingly successful exertions of the African American community in demanding their civil rights, and by judicial, congressional, and executive actions of the federal government designed to guarantee them.

The guarantee did not hold; the river flowed back on itself. It is hard to place, with accuracy, when the basic shift in the mood of the nation took place, but by 1980 it was hard upon us. Many, perhaps most, Americans expressed their resentment and rejection of all that the 1960s stood for, and that actions in the late sixties and early seventies—such as the Furman decision—initially seemed to ratify. They were determined to take back the land they thought they had lost to others who, unpatriotically, had opposed the Vietnam War, and who, by championing the civil rights of African Americans, had set free black people to take away jobs from white people.

The 1960s, it seemed to this groundswell of conservative public opinion, had put everything out of whack. Women, in an unwomanly way, had proclaimed their equality and upset the old male-dominant equilibrium. Worse still, homosexuals claimed that they too had a right to be fully regarded as people and not as aberrations. All of this was discordant to those who thought America's harmony was being drowned out. To a vast array of Americans, an established set of values undergirding a traditional way of life was perceived as being threatened.

With scorn for a frightening social upheaval, and conscious of the great increase in violent crime in the 1970s, forces of reaction went to work. Ironically, the reassertion of power was most successfully achieved in the name of the administration of justice. Nowhere has the civil rights movement made less of a difference than in the criminal justice system. Despite the gains in the legislative branches of government, the officers of the courts, prosecutors and judges, particularly on the county level where murder indictments are sought, are overwhelmingly white. The message to the African American community is that its people are still beholden to the power of the state, largely read as white. Across the land, there were moves to strengthen the authority over that sector of the populace thought to be a threat to order. Defining this group led to an immense confusion of race and class. Many of those in authority, sensing that the danger came from those who were poor and disproportionately categorizable as people of color, moved to exercise their control. Race alone had lost its edge in being the focus of majority fear. If criminals were still predominately dark, they needn't be. What was underway was the criminalization of the poor, regardless of color.

The sharpest instruments with which to threaten a threatening community were the electric chair and, increasingly, the lethal needle. In thirty-eight states, legislators passed laws restoring the death penalty, or amending old ones designed to remove the inequities disallowed by the Furman decision. It was in Georgia that a state legislature found in 1976 that they had succeeded.

In 1973, Georgia's legislature had enacted and Governor Jimmy Carter had signed a law providing new sentencing guidelines and an automatic review of the sentence by the state supreme court. That same year, Troy Gregg was convicted of murder and sentenced to death by a jury in Gwinnett County. The Georgia Supreme Court considered Gregg's appeal and upheld the judgment. Gregg's lawyer appealed the case to the Supreme Court. If the appeal were to fail, the penalty of death would once again be imposed, not solely on Troy Gregg but on those sentenced wherever fairness procedure similar to Georgia's had been enacted.

The membership on the Supreme Court had changed by only one man since the Court had rescued William Furman. William O. Douglas, the last of Franklin Roosevelt's appointees, had retired. In his place, President Gerald Ford had appointed John Paul Stevens. He would be deciding cases in a country undergoing a profound change in political morality.

The election of Jimmy Carter to the presidency later in 1976 partly disguised the fact that the nation was turning its back on liberalism. Legislators in the various states nervously awaited the outcome of the Gregg appeal. They needn't have worried. Byron White, the sole John F. Kennedy appointee to the Court— the justice who had left his foot in the door for the reentry of capital punishment in the Furman majority—found the Georgia law, and those of the other four states who joined Georgia in the Gregg case, to have satisfied him.[17]

Justice Potter Stewart, appointed by President Dwight Eisenhower, was no longer afraid of lightning. He moved from the majority that had ended the death penalty to the new majority that restored it. In Furman, he had not found capital punishment in violation of the Eighth Amendment prohibition of cruel and unusual punishment; now he wrote the opinion with which White and the four men appointed by Richard Nixon—Warren Burger, Harry Blackmun, Lewis Powell, and William Rehnquist—concurred. Burger, Blackmun, and Powell registered reluctance, but deferred to authority of the states whose legislative majorities had voted for restoration. The death penalty was back.

Capriciousness, the irrational strikes of lightning, had been cured by Georgia's new law, and the law of the land once again countenanced the death penalty. Left in gloomy disagreement were Justices William Brennan and Thurgood Marshall. Brennan, since his appointment by President Eisenhower, had become the conscience of the Court, one might even say of the nation. But it was a conscience unheeded. "This court inescapably," he wrote in dissent, "has the duty, as the ultimate arbiter of the meaning of our constitution, to say whether, when individuals condemned to death stand before our Bar, 'common moral' concepts require us to hold that the law has progressed to the point where we should declare that the punishment of death, like punishments on the rack, the screw, and the wheel, is no longer morally tolerable in our civilized society." All he could do now was to quote himself: "The fatal constitutional infirmity in the punishment of death is that it treats 'members of the human race as nonhuman, as objects to be toyed with and discarded. [It is] thus inconsistent with the fundamental premise of the Clause [Cruel and Unusual] that even the vilest criminal remains a human being possessed of common dignity.' . . . I therefore would hold . . . that death is today a cruel and unusual punishment prohibited by the Clause. . . . Justice of this kind is obviously no less shocking than the crime itself, and new 'official' murder, far from offering redress for the offense committed against society, adds instead a second defilement to the first.' "[18]

Thurgood Marshall, as a practicing trial lawyer, had kept the faith with infinitely patient optimism, pressing case after case to reach, in 1954, Brown v. Board of Education calling for the end of segregation. In time, most Americans came to accept the need to end enforced discrimination. On the Supreme Court, he had remained sanguine about the direction of the people's thinking. He had been certain that when Americans came to understand the death penalty, they would accept the Supreme Court's ending of it. Now Marshall had to admit that he was wrong: "I would be less than candid if I did not acknowledge that these developments [the enactment of the new statutes authorizing the death penalty] have a significant bearing on a realistic assessment of the moral acceptability of the death penalty to the American people."[19] But he refused to give up totally; he was convinced, in part by a survey done by political scientists, that the people still did not understand—and some day would.

Perhaps that understanding had veered from that which Marshall had been counting on. There had been a fundamental shift in the political rhetoric. The old language of compassion, unselfishness, liberality, and humanity gave way to toughness—on crime. And crime was indeed on an alarming increase in the 1970s. On into the 1980s, greed, never considered a crime, but now a virtue, became acceptable. Coupled with prideful demands for personal gain went rigid demands of conformity. Undisciplined sex and illegal drugs, it was held, had brought about a disordered social fabric and a threatening world of violence.

The enemy became the poor. Unwed mothers became not the object of charitable concern but the perpetrators of a punishable act. The blighted sections of American cities where poor people lived were seen not as places that needed help, but as gathering places for criminals. Few stopped to address the possibility that criminal acts—and there were many—were a function of the joblessness that produced this poverty.

With the cold war over and the external threat of Ronald Reagan's "evil empire" gone, Americans looked inward for domestic enemies to fear and guard against. It became dogma that the state should impose no barrier on anyone's armed self-defense. Paradoxically, this individualism was paired with a demand for the state to take a stronger role in ordering the society by passing harsher penalties for crimes. An explosion in the prison population was the inevitable result, along with a virulent insistence on the ultimate weapon. Execution of the perpetrators of the grisliest crimes would purge the land of its most threatening transgressors.

Solicitor General Robert Bork, arguing before the Supreme Court for the resumption of the death penalty and ignoring any comparison to other societies, stated that "Just as the legislature legitimately may conclude that capital punishment deters crime, so it may conclude that capital punishment serves a vital social function as society's expression of moral outrage."[20]

For him, an execution meets a communal need: A "venting of outrage at the violation of society's most important rules—'retribution' perhaps, although stripped of its vindictiveness—is itself an important, perhaps a necessary, social function. . . ." For Justice Marshall, it was the death penalty itself that violated society's rules. He knew that the death penalty did not deter crime and saw its restoration as a matter of a terrible swift sword.

Donald D. Matthews, historian of American religion, has formulated a bold thesis to account for our embrace of vengeful justice. He turns away from the traditional view that our unique enthusiasm for the death penalty was a legacy of frontier justice. Instead, focusing on lynching, but recognizing the applicability of his thesis to the death penalty, he finds Americans responding to the concept of a wrathful God and death as a means of atonement. As he puts it with respect to the worst years of lynching, the 1890s, "religion and lynching were waxing in influence in [the South] at the same time." The same could be said of the present era, with its outspoken calls for both a stern brand of religion and the death penalty.

Punishment "was sacralized by the dominant religion of the

American South" a century ago, and it is being so sacralized again now. In "God Without Thunder: An Unorthodox Defense of Orthodoxy," Matthews notes that John Crowe Ransom's "god was the 'stern and inscrutable God of Israel' rather than the liberals' 'amiable and understandable God,' " a God of compassion. In a Christianity positing original sin, redemption could only be achieved by God giving His son to "die for our sins." "At the heart of salvation were the metaphors of retributive justice: at the center was a symbol of torture and death; the word for Christ's saving action [on the Cross] was 'atonement.' "[21] So imbued with this belief system were some adherents of lynchings—and now executions—that for them, only with a killing can we atone for the sins of the society or one of its worst miscreants.

Those adhering to an opposite concept of religion—one based on forgiveness—are committed to the proposition that even the greatest of sinners can be redeemed through a process of rehabilitation. This view is not presently in the ascendancy, but the idea that we do not have it in our moral power to speak for God and inflict death either singly or societally is not held by liberal theologians alone. In a conversation with a Baptist housepainter, I asked why he opposed the death penalty when so many in his denomination championed it? He replied that "two wrongs don't make a right." Rejecting the "eye for an eye" of Old Testament law, he stated, with unabashed conviction, that since "the birth of Our Lord, Jesus Christ, we live in a state of grace; there is forgiveness now; we do God's will." But we may not interpret that will for him; He alone can decide about a death.[22]

BITS OF THESE ideas charged through my head as I drove along the country road into a darkening evening. That day I had seen people at work in defiance of the fears so prevalent in our America. By the time I reached Athens, I knew that I had to write something about the lawyers who were actively engaged in trying to save a man's life. It would be the account, too, of their clients, who, having taken a life, still wanted to save their own.

Back in Athens, I sat down the next morning and wrote a letter to Stephen Bright, saying that I hoped to tell such a story, but would only do so if it would not impede his work. I added that if I were to write such a book, I would need access to some of the office's papers. After letting the letter age over the weekend, I drove down to the post office and slipped it nervously into the out-of-town slot. By return mail, Bright, who knew little about me, responded that he would welcome my writing about their work and inviting me to come in and get to work. In the first break from classes three weeks later, I was up early to try to beat the lanes of interstate traffic into downtown Atlanta and find his office.

4

83 Poplar Street

THE NARROW THREE-story city building, crisp white facing over brick, marked, simply, "83," is folded into a row of buildings on an Atlanta street as slim as an alley. After parking, I rang the bell and was buzzed in. MaShelle Epps, the receptionist, smiled a greeting while answering the ringing phone with just two words: "Law Offices." Formally, this is the Southern Center for Human Rights, but that has too much heft for how things go here.

I was in the door for the first of many visits that fall and winter. As I came to know the place and the people, the remarkable personality of 83 Poplar Street took shape. I have seen some of the grander New York City law offices; this one is like them only in that the air is saturated in the law. I recall solemnity at mahogany desks in New York; you feel somehow here at the center that there is no emotional time for forced decorum. If millions of dollars hang on a case in New York, a single life does in Atlanta. If in corporate law's richly carpeted halls a client is lost one day, the loss can be corrected the next. There is not much that is correctable about a corpse.

For Stephen Bright's group, simply digging into a case no matter what the odds of success is the only way to achieve a rescue. Every inch of 83 Poplar's modest space is put to the task. The small rooms are arranged dumbbell fashion, two in back, two in front, with slim middle rooms along narrow halls. The walls are hung with only the most handsome of framed Amnesty International and anti–death penalty posters. Good taste runs breathlessly to keep up with good causes. Nothing without a worthy message is allowed in. A neatly framed collage of scores of passport-sized photographs of men before their executions in Virginia is a slap in the face; but not even that is allowed to bring on anything but determination.

MaShelle, her hair close-cropped on a handsome head, her body lean and elegant, is in command of the imperious telephone–public address system. At the moment, she's summoning Palmer Singleton for a call. Just across the hall the office manager, Julia Jackson, dignified and cordial, keeps the chaos under remarkable control. These two counterbalance the sartorial disarray upstairs. A small law library shares the first floor with pigeonholes for mail; an awe-inspiring copying machine; a nook for a miniature icebox and the usual makings for coffee; and a bathroom. Tanya Greene, the Blackmun Fellow, is poring through a volume of statutes at the library table.

When Tanya and I sit down for a restless, candid talk, I learn just how deceptive was her demure manner in Judge Newton's courtroom back during the Carzell Moore hearing in McDonough. Tanya was born in New York City, but the Greene family moved to Memphis and she went to Central High School, from which so many remarkable African American students have come. After graduating in 1987, Tanya went on to Wesleyan University in Connecticut. With college behind her, she taught in a preschool program for poor children on the West Coast.

Tanya's father never went beyond fourth grade, which was standard, she says, for black people when he was growing up in Memphis. She remembers her father's days as an environmental activist (before there were environmental activists) fighting to stop the backup of sewage into a local school. He never could get a lawyer to help him. (He would have made a good one himself, she feels.) "You love to talk, to argue," he told Tanya, "you'd make a great lawyer."[1] She came to think he had the right idea, that the "best tool" to use on social justice issues was the law. And so she went to Harvard Law School.

There Tanya found "plenty of white liberals around," but Charles Ogletree was the professor she turned to: "It matters more to me to find black people who make sense. . . ." She studied housing law and Indian law and spent a summer on a reservation. "Once I realized you could make up your own 'clinical' [independent study involving field work], I made up quite a few, and 'Tree would just sign off on 'em. I worked in prisons with women when there were no classes." Tanya doesn't see herself as "some kind of rich, famous, wonderful, philanthropist. . . . I'm just a basic person," she reports with a rich, musical laugh.

Early on, she knew what work she wanted to do: "I had a cousin who was faced with a death penalty at one point. . . . It's been in the family—always talked about, part of the bigger picture. . . . I don't come from any money, don't have any interest in any money." Some people from the working class "go for the big money; some of us live from hand to mouth, which is what we're doing here." (Everyone at the center from cellar to ceiling gets paid no more than $23,000 a year.)* In her third year, she took Stephen Bright's death penalty course: "He solicited me big time; I don't know why, but he did. I didn't want to come back to the South. . . . I didn't know what I was doing."

She does now. "I love my work. . . . I've had a couple wins." In one case, two months after she got here, "I did a hearing—by myself," she reports, again with a peal of laughter. "I didn't know what I was doing . . . but we won [a new trial]." When it's

---

*Funds for the center come solely from private sources. Fund raising is done by Stephen Bright and members of the Board of Directors, headed by Professor Charles Ogletree of the Harvard Law School.

scheduled, she will try it. She's proud too of her rapport with
black clients—black lawyers are rare coming onto death row
and black women lawyers even more so—and, guardedly, Tanya
tells of missing that easy connecting in an office in which, for a
moment, she was the only African American lawyer.

Nothing at 83 Poplar Street is dreary and nothing dear; in the
bathroom a patch of the wall's brick shows through behind the
rack holding extra toilet paper, but there are no hanging ferns to
duck. The walls are white because "that's what you do with
walls."[2] In the hallway is a gaudy collection of colored photographs, the faces of law students who have worked here as summer interns grinning across at each other. Bryan Stevenson, the
office's most illustrious alumnus, is not hard to spot. He was an
intern in 1983 and 1984 when he was at the Harvard Law
School, joined the staff the following year, and stayed for four
years before moving to Alabama. In 1989, Stevenson, now in
charge of a capital defense center in Alabama, was representing
Walter McMillian—he is known as Johnny Dee—a black man
convicted for murder and awaiting execution. Stevenson did his
own detective work; he was suspicious of the evidence that had
convicted McMillian.

With his findings in hand he successfully appealed to the
Alabama Court of Criminal Appeals, which to his surprise, in
1993 ordered a new trial.[3] It was never held; the prosecutor con-
ceded that McMillian had been convicted on perjured testimony and dropped all charges. The rare reversal of a black man's
death sentence in Alabama earned Stevenson nationwide attention. For this case and his other death penalty work, Stevenson
was awarded a MacArthur Fellowship. He used the funds to
support his Equal Justice Initiative in Montgomery, which provides legal support for those on death row and other indigent
clients.

Number 83 Poplar Street has been home for the Bright team
since 1990. It was only an inexpensive shell before the move;
Bright used donated funds and his imagination to achieve its
simple freshness. Once a neighbor's exterior wall, the center's

staircase wall was left bare to the bricks. Stencils still advertise
in bold but interrupted script, RHETT O'BEI . . . . 'S I[nsur]ANCE
AGENCY, once down the street at 33 Poplar. Slanting up the let-
tered brick are gray metal banisters and open stairs rising to the
two floors above and descending to the cellar.

At the foot of the stairs to the cellar, Tamara Theiss, an investigator, has an office that is literally a hole in a wall, carved into
the rock under Atlanta. Tamara, I discover, was responsible for
the Grand Dragon's appearance at the Moore hearing. When the
lawyers decided that the celebrations at Roosevelt Green's execution were relevant to his co-defendant, Carzell Moore's, case, the
investigators at 83 Poplar Street, using newspaper accounts of the
events outside the Jackson death chamber, set out to track down
those present there and afterward at a party in a bar in Macon.

Theiss, a dangerously luscious, blond young woman, went to
the bar, hoping to find the huge sign that had been printed in the
paper as advertising the party in blatant racist terms. "I really
shouldn't have been there; not exactly the safest place in the
world." She got a "very cold reception; it was clear that I wasn't
wanted." She left without the sign.

Another picture in the paper had shown Edward Stephens in
full Klan regalia. Stephens, she discovered, lived in Jonesboro,
just south of Atlanta. She had a phonebook address, and turning
off the interstate she had no trouble finding the house: "I had
never seen such a huge Confederate flag [as the one] on a flag-
pole in his front yard; it was just huge.

"I just knocked at the door . . . the amazing thing was he just
let me right in. . . . He was totally prepared [to talk]." They sat
down and discussed Stephens's philosophy of the death penalty
as he told of the many executions, black and white, that he had
attended. He was eloquent; "it was all very civilized. He was
happy as a clam to talk to me." All of this surprised Theiss, who
had been expecting she would have to serve her subpoena as she
was being thrown out of the house—or off the porch. Instead, the
Grand Dragon was happy to come to the hearing and have another chance to express his ideas in public.

In the cellar itself, next to Tamara's office, the walls are lined
with racks holding storage boxes full of files, each marked simply with a last name. These boxes contain the records of cases
that have absorbed the attention of the people upstairs. Nearby,
file cabinets hold inch-thick depositions and transcripts of the
trials and of persons whose cases are now closed. When later I
begin searching through these drawers and boxes of lives lived,
lost, sometimes rescued, I find that the boxes are full of newspaper clippings that bring back the immediacy of the details of
the formal records.

In one box, along with a Bible, a New Testament, and unsent
letters asking for help from lawyers all over the country, each
written in a careful hand on yellow pads with a ballpoint pen, is
the six-page typed memorandum outlining the rules of behavior
for those USD—Under Sentence of Death. There are photographs and letters from prison, often intimate and distant at the
same time, addressed to (and answered by) people at 83 Poplar
Street. Oddly alive here in these boxes in the cellar, and in the
photographs tacked up over desks upstairs, are the clients for
whom these offices exist. "Amadeo" and "Brooks" were the
names on a good many boxes; I was to spend a great deal of time
foraging in the boxes of those two clients.

Before descending to the cellar and some research, I had
been up to the third, the top floor, to see Stephen Bright, Palmer
Singleton, and Charlotta Norby, and the chief investigator, Mary
Eastland. Palmer is in one of the rear office rooms with only a
high-up dungeon window.

Palmer grew up in the steel city of Gary, Indiana, and retains
his gravelly midwestern voice. His parents are Quakers, as is
Staughton Lynd, the radical antiwar protester running the
Writers' Workshop in Chicago who became important in
Singleton's life. The workshop was a meeting place for those
committed to basic change in the society, specifically in the
steel workers' union. While still in his teens, Singleton worked
with the group, and in college at the University of Chicago he
thought of becoming a historian, as Lynd had.

History caught up with Singleton. Repelled by the Vietnam War, he refused to register for the draft and was sent to prison. "I couldn't get books in prison, and U of C couldn't care less," but professor Gerda Lerner and the short story writer Grace Paley interceded, got books to him, and later achieved his release from prison. Next, Palmer went to New York University Law School—not, he claims, to become a practicing lawyer, but to ready himself for work in labor education.

At NYU, he was influenced by another radical, Graham Hughes, who led him into criminal law. He has been practicing and teaching it ever since. George Kendall, once in the office with Singleton and no slouch of a lawyer himself, says Palmer has a truly brilliant mind. Often when Kendall faces a tricky case, he turns to Singleton, who "always has an imaginative response." The IQ level at 83 Poplar Street is high, but it is likely that no one tops Singleton's penetrating intellect.

When, pipe in hand, Palmer steps out of 83 Poplar Street, it is to walk up the block to the office's local eatery, the Tasty Town. A denizen of this refuge for 11th Circuit left-wingers, Singleton knows all the gossip of Gus and his crew, whose cheerful ministrations are on a level somewhat above the quality of the cuisine. But once, for a celebration at 83, a fine baklava appeared as a surprise.

An intensely private person, Palmer is totally committed to his dogs; there is Tamara Theiss and other friends in his life, but no person stands ahead of his animals. Palmer cohabits a tiny Grant Park house with a half-dozen plus Siberian huskies and a German shepherd, who rule the premises, which include an elaborately fenced yard. Singleton pays far greater attention to the medical problems of these huskies than he does to his own health. Despite occasional seizures following brain surgery for hemorrhaging, Singleton toughs it out rather than succumb to any sensible preventive regimen.

Palmer Singleton knew Stephen Bright in Washington before either of them wound up at the Southern Center. He came in 1983 to help out for six months; he stayed six years. But, in

1989, after two vexing trials of defendants—"one was the best client on earth, the kind you live and die for; the other was the worst client on earth"—he left abruptly. It appears that the same result—both escaped execution and received life sentences—for two people so apart shook this lawyer, more sensitive than his exterior exposes, to the point of needing to get away to think clearly.

For two years, Palmer taught at the State University of New York in Buffalo. He came back to the center in 1991 and talks of his clients as individuals, not as a class of aberrant beings, a group description he refuses to accept. "All too often my clients are all too normal, and all too usual . . . banal; a few are admirable, heroic; fewer . . . are despicable." Singleton is as much a mainstay of the center's litigation as Stephen Bright.

Next door is Mary Eastland, something of a wonder. As thin as a pencil—lunch seems usually to be a cold baked potato—save on days in court, she wears T-shirts always proclaiming a good cause. And every cause is championed with posters and clippings on her office walls. Her unabashed expressions of sympathy for those wronged by society are sometimes wearing on someone of Singleton's gruffness. (The response is recipro-cated, though the two very different people are fond of each other.) But an emotional take on life does not signal a mushy mind; Eastland is a smart, cagey investigator, with an eye for the telling fact about a potential witness or juror she is checking out.

Mary Eastland was short only of her dissertation in her pur-suit of a doctorate in history at Florida State University when she turned her prodigious talent for research to work on such projects for the center as the study of the racial composition of Georgia juries on which she testified at the Moore hearing. Her diffidence of manner toward men in authority, remaining from before the feminist movement disallowed it, is more than matched by a to-the-point mind that does that movement proud.

Eastland, who stems from an old southern family whose stands on racial issues she has repudiated, is nonetheless the perfectly mannered lady in her dealings with those she interviews, often disarmingly. And fervor dominates when she and her longtime partner, activist Lewis Sinclair, who serves on the center's board, attend a march for civil rights or a death watch vigil outside the Jackson prison. Mary is indefatigable in keeping up the center's correspondence with its clients in prison and with allies in the fight against capital punishment outside the legal world.

In the next office down the hall sits Charlotta Norby, a pale beauty, antique earrings dangling, with the elegance of a Vanessa Redgrave. She is a native of Denmark; the Danes, like most other Europeans, cannot believe that the United States still has the death penalty. France, Germany, the Scandinavian countries, Spain, Ireland—the list goes on—all have taken it off the books.*

Charlotta is another former intern who, after law school at New York University, came back to the center. The personal as well as professional partner of Steve Bright, she had all of 83 Poplar Street rooting for her when she suffered a ruptured aneurysm of the brain. There was great relief when she survived, but the aftereffects have, for a time, curtailed her courtroom work. It is not long before I learn that Charlotta, like Mary, holds a good deal of the history of the group's cases in her head.

Up front, Stephen Bright is in his office. Tacked onto the wall above his battered desk are scores of colored snapshots of his clients. Some, like the one of William Brooks and him, arms around each other's shoulders, or those of other young men surrounded by a parent or two, a brother or a sister, are the most conventional of commencement pictures; one proud man even wears a mortarboard. I'm told he is Tony Amadeo. The only difference is that here what is being recorded is the beginning of a lifetime in jail.

The smiles on the black faces—more are black than white—

---

*In January 1999, the United Kingdom, by signing the Sixth Protocol to the European Convention on Human Rights, formally abolished the long-dormant death penalty. Russia is expected to do so later in the year.

reflect the relief that the man in the center has not been put to death. The cause for celebration is that there will be such a life-time. Like the others on this floor, Bright would balk at the term "senior"; they see themselves as such only in having been at the job a good many more years than their younger colleagues. If there is genuine egalitarianism in a group including MaShelle at the telephone and the brilliant lawyers who bray into their speakerphones when she tells them to, there is nothing to pre-vent the exercise of a dominant personality. Stephen Bright's fills the place to overflowing. His clear, friendly, strong voice, punctuated by a deep chuckle, pours out an endless stream of accurate recollections on his clients' cases.

These clients are not defined by some category—condemned murderers, or death row inmates—but are individuals with dis-tinct personalities. Tony is not William; neither of them is like Carzell, or any of the others. And, as Bright puts it, they "are more than the worst thing they did in their lives."[4] These people committed crimes that warrant the full cluster of synonyms for "despicable," but those lives have continued. That continuation, in fact, is precisely what the law offices are all about.

Bright is all over 83 Poplar. He leaps out of his chair to trot down the stairs to Xerox some newspaper clippings; to the cel-lar to haul transcripts that will make a pile two feet high on the floor next to a desk in an office that I have borrowed. Putting me at ease, he puts me to work—as he does everyone else; his own work schedule seems to allow for no breaks. In fact, as you come to know Steve Bright, you wonder if, in his ceaseless quest to achieve the continuance of life for others, he isn't careless with his own.

Since he had a heart attack when he was still in his twenties, Bright's friends worry about his health. A while back his col-leagues in the office, thinking he needed exercise and knowing he liked to swim, gave Steve a membership in the YMCA. He swam a few times, stopped going regularly, and the membership lapsed. His earliest swimming had been as a boy on the farm outside Danville, Kentucky. In college at the University of

Kentucky he was as active as he is now; deeply involved in both the civil rights and antiwar movements, he was president of the student body in the momentous spring of 1970.

He stayed in Lexington for law school. His first job was in the rural Appalachian Research and Defense Fund, whose director, John Rosenberg, provided an extraordinary example of working with indigent clients. With a big leap in geography, Bright moved to the Public Defender's Office in Washington, D.C., where he also headed a program that brought some of the capital's many law students in to work with poor defendants.

Getting Bright alone in his office, I ask him to tell me how he got into this work. "I can talk," he answers. I knew that; "artic-ulate" is a word that defines Bright. Wondering if there might be a little something more to it, he responds, "I grew up during the sixties . . . when people were more concerned about this sort of thing . . . there was an excitement and commitment around the civil rights movement . . . the greatest time in the world. [A] lot of people grew out of it. I just never did, never matured." He chuckles.

"My dad is a farmer, dirt farmer, and he was strongly of the view that it was wrong to treat people differently because of the color of the their skin." This was risky in rural Kentucky. And "there was a minister, George Chauncey—I grew up in the Presbyterian Church—who really challenged the church not to just sit there and sing songs on Sunday, but to go out and actu-ally do something about race discrimination, do something about poverty. You can imagine how that was welcomed in the church; I mean, they literally ran the man out of town. It didn't seem to me that we were exactly living out the Sermon on the Mount there in Danville. . . . As long as I can remember, my goal was to do something that would make a difference."

He has done so, as not a few men, once on death row, can attest. But the personal price is high. Although Bright affects an all-in-a-day's-work approach, there can be no doubt that experi-encing two executions in one week is wrenching. After a final appeal in the Joseph Carl Shaw case in South Carolina, Steve spent the last day with "J.C., walking with him to the execution chamber," and was there as Shaw was strapped into the electric chair and killed. Immediately afterward, with almost no sleep, Bright was on a plane to Florida, after another final appeal had failed, to repeat the draining experience of staying with James David Raulerson until his death.

There has been little time for much else. Two marriages have failed. He has no children—in his and Charlotta's comfortable house, pictures of other people's children are everywhere—and time for almost no escape into the world of music or even reading that is not connected to his work. A vacation, even to Europe, is apt to coincide with a paper researched and prepared to be given at a conference on the death penalty. The tug of family is still there; he is close to his father, who has severe health problems, back in Kentucky. Recently he was about to go home for the high school graduation of a favorite nephew when he got word that the boy had been killed in an automobile accident. He and Charlotta hurried to the farm outside Danville; the toll on him was almost as great as on his sister and the boy's father.

Not even such personal tragedy can slow Bright down or diminish his endless articulation of his battle against the death penalty. For this, Bright still uses the rhetoric of his 1960s; for him, as for more Americans than conservatives prefer to notice, it still has life. I wondered how others here like Tanya in law school in the very different 1990s would talk about their path into this work. To find out, I went to the second floor to see Chris Johnson and Robin Toone.

From their offices, you look across Poplar Street at the shoulder of the massive granite mausoleum that is the federal courthouse. It is named for Elbert Tuttle, a former army general appointed to the court by President Eisenhower. Tuttle was one of the remarkable handful of white southern 5th Circuit Court of Appeals judges who, during the civil rights movement, made crucial, unpopular decisions that fundamentally changed the legal standing of black Americans.

Tuttle died in 1996, at age ninety-eight, and there are few

echoes today of his powerful words in behalf of the powerless in the building named for him. He had, in fact, already seen the Supreme Court turn away from an extension of his compassionate concept of the law when, in 1979, he took action to stop the first execution since that Court had permitted the resumption of the death penalty. Concluding in 1976 that Georgia's legislature had enacted procedures that would correct the abuses that made the Court end the death penalty four years earlier, they had authorized the state to execute Troy Gregg.

Troy Gregg had been put on death row, but he did not stay there; he was one of the prisoners who escaped from the supposedly secure Reidsville prison, home of the electric chair. His freedom was short-lived; Gregg was shot and killed in a bar, reportedly in a fight over a woman. The escape of dangerous criminals did not dim enthusiasm for the death penalty in Georgia. But, as late as 1979, no one who resisted had been executed. (In Utah, Gary Gilmore, who had murdered a service station attendant and a motel clerk, had asked to be shot and was.)[5]

A key provision of Georgia's new law was that all death sentences would be reviewed by the state's supreme court. Opponents of the death penalty, running after a departing bus, hoped that scrupulous attention by the various highest state courts would result in few, or perhaps none, of the sentences being upheld. Their hopes pulled away from them with a defiant screech of the brakes.

The departure took place in Florida when John Spenkelink was executed. His lawyer, David Kendall, a Rhodes Scholar and Yale Law School graduate, was a white civil rights worker in Mississippi in 1964; he was arrested eight times during his first six weeks in the state. As a clerk to Justice Byron White, Kendall heard Anthony Amsterdam argue eloquently in the Furman case that the death penalty should be ended. Kendall himself contributed to that goal by winning another Georgia case, Coker v. Georgia, in 1977, which ended the death penalty for rape. But the 1976 Gregg decision, restoring the death penalty, meant there was more work to do. At the National

Association for the Advancement of Colored People's Legal
Defense and Educational Fund, Kendall handled several cases
that did not result in the death penalty. Then, in Florida, he took
the case of John Spenkelink.[6]

There had been immense pressure on Florida governor Bob
Graham, once a foe of the death penalty. Amnesty International
led a worldwide campaign urging that Graham be merciful to the
condemned man. Though said to be agonizing over a grant of
clemency, the governor, as one of the new breed of southern
Democrats with reconstructed racial views, thought it essential
to balance that stance with a toughness on crime. To hold him
fast to that resolve, Graham's fellow young governor, Bill Clinton
of Arkansas, called with legal advice, lest Graham make a mis-
take and jeopardize the restoration of the death penalty in other
states.[7] There were thousands of letters and phone calls in
Spenkelink's behalf. Graham, as unyielding as the courts that
were appealed to, signed the death warrant.

It was then that Judge Tuttle was approached. Kendall had
been joined in these final desperate efforts by two men: Millard
Farmer, a Georgia lawyer who had, almost singlehandedly,
warded off all efforts at execution in his state; and former
Attorney General Ramsey Clark from Texas. With less than six
hours before the Florida electric chair would be back in action,
Farmer and Clark met in Atlanta and, late in the evening, went
to Tuttle's house.

Farmer laid out the facts of the case. Clark spoke "passionately," stressing that Spenkelink was facing execution for a
purely political reason: He was a white man, whose death
"would inoculate Florida from 150 years of racial discrimination
in capital cases." Tuttle, listening "solemnly" as Clark spoke,
"took a deep breath" and signed a hastily drawn order for a stay
of execution.[8]

Spenkelink, his head and left leg already shaved in preparation, was taken from the room adjacent to the electric chair and
returned to his cell for the harrowing wait while the lawyers
prayed that Tuttle's full 5th Circuit Court would not vacate his

stay and that the Supreme Court would not vacate another stay independently applied for and signed by Justice Thurgood Marshall.

Both stays were indeed vacated—before Governor Graham's death warrant expired. After yet another last night, John Spenkelink "walked"—deadly slang for the shackled shuffle into the execution chamber. He was strapped into the electric chair; twice, the voltage of the notorious Florida electric chair failed to kill. On the third try it completed its job. His left leg smoking, Spenkelink died on May 25, 1979.

It is just such state killings that Chris Johnson has been trying to prevent since graduating from the Harvard Law School in 1994 and clerking, briefly, for Alan B. Handler, a justice on the New Jersey Supreme Court who is opposed to the death penalty. Johnson had spent two summers working in the then federally funded capital punishment resource centers providing counsel to death row inmates in South Carolina and Mississippi; another was spent teaching in a Gaelic language summer camp in Ireland. He came to the center in the fall of 1995.

Chris's background is very different from that of Tanya Greene, Palmer Singleton, or Stephen Bright. He comes from a California family; his father, a corporate lawyer, is an advocate of equal housing. His mother would take Chris with her to test fair housing practices when a woman of color, with a child, had been turned down and prejudice was suspected. It was a highly comfortable liberal upbringing without the contact with the other side of the law that was family knowledge for Greene. There is an old-guard reserve in Chris; talk of motives and emotions comes hard. But both are deeply seated within him.

Robin Toone has the other front office on the second floor. A big, friendly bear of a man, Robin seems easy to know. It isn't long before he confesses that he went into law school—Yale, in his case—with the intention of doing indigent defense work and came out, as many others did not, enacting his intention. Toone's interest in the death penalty goes back to a course taught in his residential college during his Yale undergraduate years by two graduate law students, Michael Barr at Yale, and Dan Abrahamson at New York University.

In his first year in law school, Toone begged his way into Steve Bright's course—taught, unfashionably, with a "tenacious" requirement that students argue as prosecutors as well as good-guy defense lawyers, and hold up under the teacher's relentless queries. He had the students right there in the courtroom, not in a debate over law review articles, and Bright's "passion was always there" as he peppered student after student with tough questions. Time wasn't wasted on "liberal bromides— race is wrong." There was not much in the way of the immense complexities of habeas corpus law that they could escape learning. As the course ended, Bright's parting words were, "See you in the courts."

According to Toone, Bright was untypically informal in his relations with his students—eating supper with them, conversing (loudly, cheerfully) in the halls of the law school. There was method in his manner. As a teacher, he is always proselytizing— as Tanya, too, had learned. More lawyers are needed to fight the death penalty. But, interestingly, when Toone signed on to work at 83 Poplar the fall after graduation, he was set to work on the civil rights questions raised by Georgia's prison conditions, work he also had been drawn to in a clinical program in law school that provided legal services for prisoners.*

Leaving Robin's office, I walk past the second-floor bathroom with its tiny stall shower ready for a lawyer needing, some morning, to shed casual clothes and change into a suit for a trip to

---

*Robert Bensing joined Toone at the center in late 1995 to join in the prison conditions work. In 1998, he won a settlement from the state after bringing charges, substantiated by testimony from guards and counselors, against the Commissioner of Corrections, Wayne Garner, for witnessing, indeed supervising, the beating of unresisting prisoners by other guards in two of the state's prisons. The afternoon before the settlement was announced in *The New York Times*, Bensing, who had been visiting two clients in another prison in South Georgia, was killed in an automobile accident on an interstate highway as he was driving back to Atlanta. Stephen Bright gave the eulogy at this memorial service, which Commissioner Garner, still in office, attended.

court, or—far into the night—waking up to keep going with the brief at hand. Lawyers as a breed (eager young ones, at least) make a fetish of sleeplessness, but that is carried to obsession here.

On one of my first visits to the center, I ran into Chris Johnson arriving early in jeans and a sweater. Later, looking up from a pile of transcripts, I saw him rushing out in crisp white shirt, bright tie, and suit. His ornery hair slicked back, he was straight out of GQ and off to Birmingham for a hearing in Kenny Smith's death penalty case—Chris's first.

5

Birmingham, Alabama

IN 1988, THE Reverend Charles Sennett, tired of his wife and having found a replacement, but fearing that a divorce would cost him his pulpit, engaged a young man, Billy Williams—who in turn hired Kenny Smith and a third man, John Parker—for a lump sum of a thousand dollars to kill his wife.* Williams, the broker of the deal (and the only black person involved), was not present when Kenny and the other man gained entry to the house and began beating Elizabeth Dorlene Sennett. (Kenny said he had been hired only to beat her. If so, the plan had changed.)

Elizabeth Sennett admitted the two on their pretext that they had a message from her husband, which of course they did. In what apparently was a savage battle, she was beaten unconscious; one of them threw an afghan over her. Smith began ransacking the house to make the attack look like a robbery—and to hunt for drugs; his blood and the victim's was found on the

---

*Exchange overheard in the courtroom: "How could he have done such a thing?" "What else would you expect him to do?"[1]

mirror of a bathroom medicine cabinet. While he was gone, according to his lawyer, Parker completed the beating, accomplished with fireplace tools, a wooden cane, and a wooden stool, by stabbing her to death through the afghan.

When the police discarded the robbery theory, their suspicion turned to the good reverend. He committed suicide. The three conspirators were arrested. In separate trials, all three were found guilty. Billy Williams, the organizer, received a life sentence. John Parker was sentenced to death and is still on death row. Kenny Smith was also found guilty of murder and Judge N. Pride Tompkins sentenced him to death. During his time in prison and away from drugs, Smith proved a different person. He turned to religion and counseled other prisoners; one inmate confided that Kenny had helped him confront his homosexuality: "There is nothing I can't go to him with and if he can provide it he will. He was the best friend I had in my life. . . . I trust him with my life."[2]

The then federally funded Alabama Resource Center turned to the Southern Center (which has had many cases in Alabama, as well as Georgia) to provide assistance to two conscientious but inexperienced court-appointed lawyers for an appeal. Charlotta Norby took the case. She argued that prospective African American jurors had been dismissed by the prosecutor for no reason other than race. This the Supreme Court forbade, adding, in 1991, that it did not matter if the defendant was, as Kenneth Smith is, white. It was the right of jurors to fulfill their responsibility as citizens that was at issue, and they could not be prevented from exercising it simply for reasons of race or gender.

Heeding her, the Alabama Court of Criminal Appeals ordered the matter back to Judge Tompkins. He held a hearing at which the prosecutor could not come up with valid, nonracial reasons for the exclusion of the dismissed jurors. To Norby's surprise, Tompkins ruled that the prosecutor had indeed deliberately kept African Americans off the jury. As a result, Tompkins is to preside over another murder trial for Kenny Smith.

Kenny had confessed, and his lawyers had their work cut out for them. Assuredly, Mrs. Sennett had been killed. Under Alabama law, which provides a strict definition of capital murder, Kenny had to have intended to kill her if he was to be convicted of that crime for which, alone, a death sentence could be imposed. The alternative punishment for such a crime in Alabama was a sentence of lifetime imprisonment, without the possibility of parole. But, without intent, it would be felony murder, with a sentence allowing for parole.

Smith's first trial in 1989 was moved to Birmingham from rural Colbert County where the killing took place and where emotions still rode high. Judge Tompkins moved with the case then and presided again in April 1996 at Smith's second trial, which Palmer Singleton argued with the assistance of Charlotta Norby and Chris Johnson. In the trial, Singleton, as is usual, chose not to call the defendant, in order to prevent his being cross-examined, concentrating instead on challenging the state's twelve witnesses.

One state witness, Ralph Earl Robinson, told of going with his wife to Kenny Smith's house expecting to go out celebrating. Kenny said he didn't have the money to go out; they agreed to stay home and play cards. Eventually, the two men went off to get some whiskey; on the way, Kenny "kept saying how he messed up. And I said, what are you talking about? He said, I can't say, I don't want to get you involved. I said, well, leave it alone then."[3]

During the card game, Robinson recalled, Kenny began crying. "I asked him did he need to talk. He said, yeah," and the two men went out into the front yard. Smith—"he was upset real bad"—told his friend of the attack on Mrs. Sennett: "I said, you know you messed up, didn't you? He said, yeah. I said, it might be easier on you if you go turn yourself in, and he just looked at me real funny."[4] Other friends of Smith were called to testify, and in his cross examination, Singleton sought to establish that Smith had been hired to beat up the woman, not to kill her.

There was virtually no hope for an outright acquittal, the goal was a conviction for less than capital murder. Convincing the jury that there was, on Smith's part, no intent to kill was the lawyers' job. The one thing the lawyers had going for them—and more crucially for Smith—was the composition of the jury. In Birmingham's Jefferson County, the list of prospective jurors is available to attorneys only immediately before the day on which the defense lawyers and prosecutors get to inquire into the jurors' knowledge of the case, their views on relevant issues in order to challenge some, seat others. Singleton, Norby, and Johnson could not make use of the investigators in the office to establish the backgrounds of citizens of the county called for potential duty.

No matter. Whether because of Singleton's astute questioning or pure luck—or the fact that the prosecutor was exceedingly wary of challenging any African American jurors—they wound up with twelve conscientious, alert jurors. But, like most jurors, they knew little of the law they had the dread duty of implementing other than what the judge would spell out for them.

Smith's only chance was that the jury would not find that he intended to kill Sennett. The chance was lost when the judge, in a rambling, unclear charge to the jury, obscured the issue of intention. Once again a jury convicted Kenny Smith of capital murder, and at that point, in Alabama, as Singleton puts it, you "might as well get out the shovel and start digging." Despite the long tradition of the primacy of the jury, and the fact that in the federal and greater number of state jurisdictions a unanimous decision is necessary for the death penalty to be imposed, in four states—Alabama, Florida, Delaware, and Indiana—a jury's decision on the death penalty is only advisory; the judge can ignore the advice. (In several other states, including Arizona, Idaho, and Montana, the jury does not participate in the decision on punishment at all.)[5] In Georgia, it takes only one juror to hold out to prevent an execution.

Chris and Palmer were alone that evening with Smith in a room in the jail adjacent to the courthouse. Somehow, Chris was particularly aware of Kenny's prison clothes; he had been in coat and tie at the trial, and Chris had seen him often in jailhouse garb, but now that was the clothing that he would wear for the rest of his life. As hideous as Smith's actions had been, Chris had found that "I like Kenny." This nice-looking, well-mannered man about his own age was to Johnson distinct from the man whose record he knew so well.

Kenny Smith seemed fully to have reconstructed himself, to have irrevocably rejected the person who had participated in the assault that killed Elizabeth Sennett. That evening, following Kenny's conviction for first-degree murder, three men had to confront the reality that one of them faced a lifetime in prison, "had lost his last chance to live a life on the street and all three of us knew it." Johnson's voice dropped lower and lower as he described how he felt leaving Kenny: "He said he was in a cell with a decent human being who he could talk to. He was actually stronger than I was." I asked Chris if he broke down. "I don't think I did—then," he replied, his voice cracking as he remembered that evening.

The next morning, when the jury reconvened to consider whether Smith should receive a life sentence or be executed, Palmer rose to passionate eloquence. In the face of the prosecutor's strong examples of aggravating circumstances that he contended would justify a death sentence, Singleton had to present counterbalancing mitigating circumstances. He called Smith's brother and sister to tell of their having lived, as children, with their mother's alcoholism—how they would partially empty gin bottles and fill them with water to try to prevent her getting drunk, of Kenny at age six mopping up her vomit from the bathroom floor and helping her into bed. Singleton terms the child's action "heroic." Kenny had been reared amid serious substance abuse and, in the too familiar pattern, followed suit.

Linda Smith's drinking had followed on brutal beatings by her since-departed husband, Gene. She was a waitress, and so Chris Johnson put Vera Rushen, who had worked with Linda Smith, on the witness stand to tell how Gene Smith would come in and "take what money Linda had made in tips. And if she did not make what he thought he needed, she would get slapped and beat around right in the restaurant." Rushen went on to describe a beating and said that "that was not just one occasion, that was any time that he come around." He came in two or three times a week and there would be other beatings. In the restaurant, he would abuse her verbally, and after a beating: "she would have red bruise[s] . . . they would be red dents in her che[e]ks. He always made a point to hit her around her eyes."[6] Johnson also had Vera Rushen testify that Kenny had often witnessed these attacks.

When Kenny was about eight or nine, a third son, Michael, was born—and died while an infant. Gene Smith, blaming his wife for the baby's death, left the family for good. Linda Smith was highly reluctant to testify, to have to tell what she had so long contended to herself had never happened. Palmer Singleton impressed on her the fact that if Kenny's life were to be saved, she must do so. On the stand, she made an extraordinarily telling impression on the jury. Afterward, Mary Eastland called on one woman juror, out of an upper-class world distant from Linda Smith's and, Mary Eastland guessed, distant too in experience. Mary had expected this juror to have been repelled by the Smith story; instead, she said that she could identify totally with Linda.

Kenny Smith too had identified with his mother—and his father. He had done so in ways familiar to those who study abuse. Like his mother, he mixed Valium (and other drugs) with alcohol. So, too, he had learned the lesson of the father. He had seen his father's savage beatings cause his mother's misery— and her attempt, with drugs, to anesthetize herself. He grew up learning that the beating of a woman was a way a man could respond to desperation. He desperately needed money for an addiction of a mother and would not—could not—keep himself from replicating, fatally, the action of the father.

This had been Kenny Smith's life before the murder and culminating in it. There had been another life since. The evidence of both his childhood and his redemptive behavior in jail spoke to the jury. And so, perhaps, did one simple act of Palmer Singleton's. The prosecutor, questioning the extent of Smith's rehabilitation in prison, took note of an F in a college course that prisoners had been allowed to take. Singleton might have tried to explain the failing grade away; instead, he went over to Kenny, ran his hand through his hair, and said to him, "Get all the Fs you want"; go right on taking those courses. The jurors seeing, sensing, that one gruff, good man had accepted Smith back into the city, into the world of learning, of living, could do the same. They voted 11–1 in favor of a life sentence rather than death for Kenny.

As Charlotta Norby put it, "We could not have asked for a better jury." The lawyers allowed the family to savor the good news for a few days, and then had the task of telling them—Kenny already knew—to prepare for the worst. Under Alabama law, the family was told, the jury's vote is only advisory; it is the judge who decides whether the convicted man is to live or die.

THE FACT THAT Alabama could leave the life or death decision to one person who was free to ignore a jury recommendation when the verdict of the jury is normally insisted upon had struck many defense lawyers earlier as out of line with the consistency the Supreme Court required of death penalty procedures. To challenge the constitutionality of Alabama's practice, Ruth Friedman set to work. A small, trim, and smart New Yorker, she had made a remarkable record of death penalty cases won in Alabama since joining the center immediately after graduating from the Yale Law School in 1988. (A colleague now of Bryan Stevenson's at the Equal Justice Initiative, Friedman is credited by one expert in the field for being a key player in the rout of Alabama in its run for the record in executions.)[7]

Not many women—or men either—in their thirties argue cases before the Supreme Court, as Friedman did in Harris v. Alabama in 1994. The jury had voted to sentence Louise Harris to life in prison, but the judge had sentenced her to death. Friedman challenged this arbitrary judicial power as a violation of the Eighth and Fourteenth amendments. She lost the case, but not without moving Justice John Paul Stevens closer to opposition to the death penalty. He noted the political reality that judges in Alabama must stand for election every six years; and if they "covet higher office—or . . . merely wish to remain judges," they are likely to have to "constantly profess their fealty to the death penalty."[8] Only five times had judges spared those the jury would have condemned; forty-seven people were sentenced to die whom the juries would have spared.

For Justice Stevens, the jury, not the judge, was the voice of the community; a judge should not be permitted to ignore "the community's considered judgment . . . The absence," he continued, "of any rudder on a judge's free-floating power to negate the community's will, in my judgment, renders Alabama's capital sentencing scheme fundamentally unfair and results in cruel and unusual punishment."[9] But his were words of dissent; all eight of his fellow justices held that the decision on life or death could reside solely with Alabama judges, including Pride Tompkins.

JUDGE TOMPKINS SENTENCED Smith to death in the first trial; now, following the second, he set the date for sentencing for May 21, 1996.

On a clear day—it was going to be hot—people from the office rallied in Birmingham, to be with the client, his family, and with their colleagues. The lawyers, Charlotta, Palmer, and Chris, had left at five in the morning in order to be with Kenny before the judge's sentence. I went with Mary Eastland, who resolutely took the wheel and headed due west out of Georgia and into Alabama. With us in the car were two new interns, Marion Chartoff and Kristy Holley. The early summer green lining the highway made I-20 the classic interchangeable interstate. Nothing visible would have differentiated Alabama from Ohio or Maine as the conversation undertook to initiate a newly arrived Marion Chartoff from the Stanford University Law School into the vagaries of Alabama criminal justice. Talk became a bit more circumspect, but only a bit, as it emerged that the other new intern, Kristy Holley, from the University of Georgia, was born in Montgomery.

In Birmingham, the sun was blazing hot on the treeless concrete plaza outside the modern courthouse and jail. Mary Eastland spotted a relative of Elizabeth Sennett's arriving and saw Kenny's mother with one of his sisters and her husband, and his brother with his wife. Joining Charlotta on the plaza, it seemed best not to burden the Smiths with small talk; instead, she introduced the interns and me to Judge Tompkins, a reasonably affable and unexceptional-looking man probably in his fifties. With a disguising show of patience and decorum, we all waited restlessly for 9:30 A.M.

Downstairs in a cavernous shoebox, a windowless, paneled courtroom, the group from the office sat in a row behind the Smith family. The relatives of Mrs. Sennett were further back. At the far end of the room, the judge entered and took his seat at the bench. The deputy sheriffs brought in Kenny Smith; as they removed his handcuffs, he gave a long, searching look at his mother and brother, sitting next to her, and not with a wink but a motion with his eye made contact. Then he took his seat at the defendant's table with Charlotta, Palmer, and Chris. The district attorney sat at his.

Palmer placed only one witness on the stand, Chris Johnson, who testified on the orderly vote count on the blackboard that he had observed in the jury room immediately after the 11–1 vote. Singleton was striving to convince the judge that this was a jury that had deliberated rationally and calmly. Nodding toward three of the jurors seated in the spectators' rows, he tried to impress on the judge the force of their recommending vote. In the words of one juror, Smith "had made a tremendous change." Some people, the juror had gone on, "don't want to accept that change. That's wrong."[10]

Singleton agreed; he made a powerful statement stressing how redemptive—he used the word—Kenny's life had been beyond the terrible day of his crime. Then he rested. The district attorney chose to add nothing. All eyes, all ears were uneasily on the judge; he chose to recess until two-thirty.

Five interminable hours later, all returned. Kenny Smith's family stoically filed into their row. Kenny was brought in again, again signaled with his eye from a tense, even terror-filled face, and took his seat. The judge began to read in a voice devoid of tone the sentence on which he had settled. Palmer thought he detected a quaver in Tompkins's flat reading. Did the judge know that killing Kenny was wrong? Was reelection in an upcoming election worth a death sentence? Farther back in the courtroom, we could discern nothing of what might be in his mind. We had only his words.

What was in his statement was the fact that the assault on the victim was "for pecuniary gain." Then, as he recited the list of implements, one after another, used to kill the victim, it was clear where he would come out. Nothing was said of redemption. Judge Tompkins, spelling out the voltage, sentenced Smith to death in the electric chair and muttered: "May God have mercy on your soul."

Earlier, Palmer, expecting the worst, had come down to the pews, leaned over Mrs. Smith, whispered so closely into her ear that not even her daughter, sitting next to her, could hear, and gained her acquiescence. Then he had asked the judge if, after the sentencing, Kenny and his mother could embrace. The judge said audibly, "I'm never sure it's wise," and left it to the deputy sheriff, who gave permission. Linda Smith, having heard the sentence and knowing her son was about to be led away to await it, went forward. In full control of her emotions, she climbed the two steps to gain the level on which Kenny, still unshackled, stood. Their arms reached around each other and they were together for a long moment.

Kenny was handcuffed and taken back to jail. Out in the hall a heavy sadness hung over his mother and sister, standing tearless and still in control, waiting for a final word with Palmer. Suddenly, the door from the courtroom opened and three members of the jury, two black women and a lean, white-haired black man, came out. Lloyd Harper, Jr., without a pause, went over to Mrs. Smith and gave her a rich, enfolding hug. Her face, over his shoulder, broke from its stoic mask into a look of great gratitude.

I wanted to bolt the building, Alabama, the whole terrible business. But I couldn't. Kenny had been taken back to his cell and had to change his courtroom costume for his now-perpetual prison clothing, which he would wear until, calf shaved and bared to an electrode, his clothing would be his shroud cloaking a life that had been burned away.

Our contingent from the center had been assigned to bring the borrowed street clothes back—to be used again, perhaps, by another defendant. The wait of twenty minutes or so until a bundle was stuffed into a drawer, shoved outward, and retrieved by Mary Eastland, seemed twenty hollow hours. I offered to drive and did more damage to Alabama's legal speed than even Mary had done on the way out. Back in Atlanta, 83 Poplar Street didn't look so inviting; I got into my car and sped back to Athens.

6

Death in Columbus

THE TRIP TO Birmingham came half a year after the exploration that started when I opened the many boxes in the cellar of 83 Poplar Street marked "Brooks." I wanted to follow one case from start to finish. I had not known much of the early part of the Kenny Smith story before hearing him condemned. (Norby and Johnson have filed an appeal.) Similarly, little of the early history of Carzell Moore emerged at the pretrial hearing and his case still awaits closing. Back in the fall of 1995, in a box of the closed case of William Anthony Brooks, I found a fascinating story that predates his case. It stretches back to 1912.

After reading that mountain of transcripts that Bright had built for me, as well as newspaper accounts of William Brooks's trials and letters he wrote to Bright and Mary Eastland after they took his case, I was ready to go to the scene of the crime. Driving against the stare of oncoming lights through a waterfall of Georgia rain, on December 1, 1995, I was on the broad swath of I-85 leading to Columbus, in the far west-center of the state.

Columbus, the county seat of Muscogee County, lies one hundred miles down the Chattahoochee River from Atlanta; across the river is Alabama. In 1840, the growing city, with its iron foundries and cotton mills, built a courthouse that was a fine example of Georgia's late Federal period architecture. A beautifully proportioned four-square brick building, painted white, with a portico of Doric columns, it spoke of the republic.

In 1895, the gracious structure was pulled down; on the same site, Muscogee County built a courthouse fitting for the New South. Atlanta's Henry Grady, the spokesman for a South determined to have outsiders believe that it had put aside its old rural, slaveholding Confederate past, had decreed from the influential pulpit of the *Atlanta Constitution* that no longer should Georgia be out of step with the hoped-for prosperity of a modern capitalist America.

Not wanting to lag behind her larger sister city, Columbus would now have a courthouse of fitting substance. There were touches of New York's Stanford White in the ornamented niches on either side of five Corinthian columns that fronted the massive midsection of the building protruding from two well-proportioned flanking wings. On each wing, three pairs of tall windows above, three pairs below, were topped with curved brickwork; the generous front door opened under a complimenting curve.

Aloft on a tine rising from the dome, a graceful bronze Justice soared. The courthouse beneath was only sixteen years old when a barefoot black boy, in shorts, sat within the imposing walls of the second-floor courtroom awaiting his fate at her hands.

On the afternoon of the last day of June 1912, out on Double Churches Road eight miles north of downtown Columbus, twelve-year old Cleo Land had climbed up on a mule and rode away from the house and barn to a far-off pasture, near a stand of woods. Later in the afternoon, the mule came back to the barn—without Cleo. Apparently the boy was used to dawdling—there is a report that he may have been retarded; if so, the family had never spoken of it.[1]

When he did not come home for supper, his father, W. L.

(William Lokey) Land, suspected that Cleo might have wandered off or been thrown by the mule. With neighbors, he set out in the twilight to search for Cleo; not until 2:00 A.M. did they find his body in a ditch, covered with leaves and brush. By lantern light, it seemed at first that the boy had been kicked in the head by the mule. A closer look revealed that he had been shot.

About twelve hours earlier, out in the fields beyond his family's place, Cleo, who was white, had met up with T. Z. Cotton,* who was black. T.Z. lived in a cabin remote from the road. It appears that the boys knew each other well and were used to horsing around together. Playing with a shotgun, or, perhaps, arguing and fighting over it—T.Z. is said to have confessed that he and Cleo had been "projecting [sic] with the gun and the gun went off"—a shot hit Cleo in the head.

Terrified, T.Z. ran to the Lands' house for help, but no one was home. Coming back, he realized that Cleo was dead, and, more frightened still, he picked up Cleo's body "in his arms and carried him down and put him in the hole. He said he did it himself and no one helped him do it." Then, still dripping with Cleo's blood, he went back to his cabin, farther along on the edge of the woods, and struggled to clean the drops of blood from the cabin floor. He didn't tell anyone anything about the "accident" because he was afraid.

He had reason to be. After a funeral the next afternoon in the simple, whitewashed Mount Moriah Primitive Baptist Church, one of the pair of side-by-side churches that gives Double Churches Road its name, Cedron Cleopholus Land was buried in the Land plot in the churchyard, next to the grave of his mother, who had died the year before. Suspicion had already fallen on Cleo's playmate. Earlier that morning, July 1, a bailiff, along with the coroner, had gone to the McElhaney cabin where they found T.Z., a shotgun, and bloody clothing—and arrested the boy and brought him to jail.

---

*He was T. Z. McElhaney in the court docket, the records, and the newspapers of the day; in the black community he was—and still is—T. Z. Cotton.

That night, after the funeral, Sheriff Jesse Beard assigned seven men to stand guard "in case an attempt was made to seize the McElhaney boy."

IN COLUMBUS, WILLIAM T. Winn, a reporter and columnist for the *Columbus Ledger-Enquirer*, tells me about this long-ago murder. Billy Winn is a large, affable man who sits in his second-floor office with his chair pushed back from a wooden desk; on the wall, along with plaques and certificates for prizes won and credentials established, is a framed clipping of Julia and Julian Harris when Julian, a former publisher of the *Enquirer*, won a 1922 Pulitzer Prize for his anti-Klan editorials; a photograph of Martin Luther King, Jr.; and one of W. E. B. Du Bois. (Winn met Du Bois through his books; he hasn't, in Columbus, had much opportunity to hear his name pronounced correctly.)

Neither of the black leaders' pictures are in many white people's offices in town, but long ago I gave up being surprised by anything in the South. I'm ready when Winn tells me that as a young reporter, he covered the civil rights movement across Georgia, as well as King's funeral, for the *Atlanta Journal*, the afternoon sister paper to the *Constitution*. The *Journal* along with the *Constitution*, under its liberal editor, Ralph McGill, were voices for moderation in the South. McGill looks down from another photograph at Winn whenever he turns to his computer.

Winn came home to Columbus in 1987. As much historian as reporter, he searched his newspaper's morgue, read surviving accounts in other papers, and studied the Muscogee County records to write a thorough account of the T. Z. McElhaney trial, which he entitled "Incident at Wynn's Hill." For seven days the lengthy, detailed story ran in the *Ledger*—complete with vintage photographs. Despite diligent digging, Winn could find almost nothing, prior to the trial, on T. Z. Cotton or T. Z. McElhaney. He found no birth record and doesn't know if T. Z. Cotton was eighteen, as the prosecutor claimed, or as young as twelve, as others, who said the two boys were playmates, reported. Winn suspects the boy was close to being that young; fourteen is his best guess.

There is no explanation of why T.Z. was alone in the cabin. No relatives are reported in any of the accounts, including those of the boy's trial. Winn was unable to find any court transcripts of the trial itself, even though records of other trials of the period still exist. For his story, the reporter relied primarily on lengthy 1912 accounts in Columbus's two newspapers, the *Enquirer-Sun* and the *Ledger*.

Unaccountably, despite the quick action at the time of Cleo Land's death, T.Z.'s trial was not held until a month later in the summer. On August 5, Superior Court Judge S. Price Gilbert swore in seven bailiffs who presented evidence against McElhaney before a grand jury on which sat some of the most prominent men in the county, all of them white. Among them were W. B. Land and his cousin, R. E. L. Land, Cleo's uncle. The jury handed down an indictment of McElhaney.

The trial began on August 13 in Judge Gilbert's elaborate courtroom. In the interim between the indictment and trial, newspapers reported that Will (W. L.) Land had "visited Sheriff Beard and told him that, should the verdict be less than murder, there might be trouble." Aware of the threat, but not intimidated by it, Judge Gilbert, who had a reputation for judicial rectitude, appointed three prominent lawyers to defend McElhaney.

Judge Gilbert, along with some of the city's leading citizens, was determined that the trial would be a fair one. Columbus's reputation was already tarnished by more than its share of lynchings. This was not to be a legal lynching, a trial in which would-be lynchers were persuaded not to abduct the prisoner with the assurance the result would be a hanging.

T.Z., "barefoot and dressed in shorts and a cheap blue shirt," sat with his attorneys. Looking over to the jury box, the boy saw, among the twelve white men, the grave, white-bearded countenance of the foreman, William Beach, owner of William Beach Hardware. Staring back at T.Z. through round, dark-rimmed spectacles was J. B. Everidge, "a well-known banker and business man." A reporter present noted that the "boy did not take his eyes off those testifying or off the lawyers when they were addressing the court."

In a statement that he had given earlier, T.Z. admitted to the shooting, but said it was an accident. Asked why he didn't report it as such, he is quoted as saying: "I'm just a little black nigger and I knew that if I went to Mr. Land and told him I had killed the boy, he would kill me. I was afraid to tell him and so I hid the body." The prosecution lawyers argued that McElhaney was guilty of murder and called for the death penalty.

At five o'clock, after an hour and fifteen minutes of deliberation, the foreman of the jury told a stunned group of spectators, including Cleo's three sisters, that T.Z. was guilty not of murder but of manslaughter. Judge Gilbert then sentenced McElhaney to three years at hard labor and stepped down from the bench to start for home. The courtroom began to empty.

"The trouble began," wrote the reporter for the *Enquirer-Sun,*

> when Bailiffs R. L. Willis and J. T. Darby started to take the negro from the courtroom into the sheriff's office. Gathered in the aisles were numbers of relatives and friends of the dead boy, perhaps twenty-five in all. Suddenly the men closed around the officers and demanded the prisoner. Neither of the bailiffs were armed. They refused to surrender McElhaney and one man struck Willis in the face. Another dealt him a heavy blow and he turned the negro loose to defend himself. A strenuous fisticuff following. The negro was torn from Darby and [a] powerful man hurled the officer bodily several feet into the courthouse rotunda where the struggle had shifted by that time. Deputy Sheriff Gibson came running in and was temporarily disabled by being kicked in the stomach.
>
> In the midst of the melee, McElhaney realized what was happening and, according to an eyewitness, began to scream for protection.

None came. He was pulled out of the courthouse and across the square through a crowd of angry white people to the Tenth Street streetcar stop. When a car stopped, the men holding their victim boarded and carefully paid nineteen fares—one for T.Z. Initially, the car continued making regular in-town stops, but as they came nearer the edge of town, the other passengers were ordered off the car. One man held a pistol to the motorman's head and ordered him not to stop until he reached the city limits.

When they came to the railroad line at the foot of Wynn's Hill, they dragged T.Z., "pleading and screaming for mercy," from the car and told the motorman to go along. "Then," according to the *Enquirer-Sun* reporter, "several of the men . . . took out pistols, and the negro . . . was riddled with bullets. He uttered a cry as the first shots hit him, then fell dead." Later that day,

> Hundreds of people went out to where the negro was killed as soon as the news of the trouble became known . . . the news spread like wildfire and automobiles, motorcycles, street cars, buggies . . . were pressed into service by those who went out to the scene of the killing, as people were curious to see the work that had been accomplished by the enraged men.

After word reached the black community that the crowd had dispersed, an undertaker, Alex Toles, came out and took the body away. T. Z. Cotton was buried in the paupers' lot; no one seems to know whether in Riverdale Cemetery, as the newspapers first reported, or, as Jim Crow would have dictated, the Porterdale Cemetery. There is no marker in either.

When Billy Winn came to tell T.Z.'s story, he wrote that prayers were said and hymns sung in grief in the cabins and churches of Muscogee County's black residents. He does not, in this account, consider the anger—or the length of memory—of those people who prayed and sang. Appropriately, Winn does give the names of the prominent Columbus women and clergymen who signed a petition of protest against the lynching. He tells, too, of cries of outrage in a black Savannah paper and a white Macon paper. But it would not have been safe for the African American community in Muscogee County to speak out; the series of lynchings had done their job of intimidation. A burden of sorrow remained.

Judge Gilbert convened the grand jury to consider indictments in the murder of T. Z. McElhaney. R. E. L. Land, Cleo's uncle, and his cousin, W. Brewster Land, were excused from serving. The jurors issued a condemnation of the bailiffs and particularly Sheriff Beard for not preventing McElhaney from being taken from the courthouse and not arresting those who took him. They also handed down an indictment of murder against R.E.L., W.B., and W. L. Land (Cleo's father), and a fourth man, Lee Lynn.

Judge Gilbert presided over the trial; all four pleaded not guilty. The prosecutor would not have been short of witnesses had he exercised his power of subpoena. With so many people having business in the courthouse and in the busy square and street the day of McElhaney's trial, there were scores of witnesses to the abduction from the courthouse and a good many at the scene of the killing. When one of the defendants took the stand, he referred to Cotton as "that Negro brute," and insisted that what had transpired was justified. It took the jury twenty-nine minutes to acquit them all.

This was New South justice. With the tyranny of slavery no longer available, lynching was utilized to maintain white supremacy. With the abdication of federal enforcement of the Reconstruction civil rights amendments, there was little local justice available to black southerners. It was rare that there had even been an indictment of Cotton's killers, that they were tried. Still, they were not punished.

ON THE EVENING of my first day in Columbus, I was treated to a gourmet meal prepared by Billy Winn and his understatedly elegant wife, Elinor. Their house, handsomely spare inside, is on Front Street. From their front porch, they look out on the

Chattahoochee River; Billy's newspaper office is about five hundred yards upstream. Childhood sweethearts in Columbus—they were both born in the city—the two not only came home, but chose to live right downtown.

In the midst of a conversation that ranged far beyond Columbus, Winn returned to the Cotton case. We shared stories of the frustration of looking for evidence of events that refuses to be found. Winn had, for example, scoured the county clerk's office for the transcript of not only the McElhaney trial but also the later trial of the Lands, without luck. Records of other cases of 1912 were there, but not these.

Winn told me how well known the Lands were in Columbus; no one seems to have doubted that it was they who had taken T.Z. away and shot him. Bailiff Darby testified that it was the Lands who had seized him. A man traveling on the streetcar that day told Winn, decades later, that he realized what was happening and who the abductors were. Asked why he didn't get off the car to get help, he admitted that he was frightened: "It was the Lands. Everybody was frightened of them."[2]

A HALF CENTURY after the Cotton and Land trials, when Bill Winn was a boy, another African American was shot dead in Columbus.[3] Dr. Thomas H. Brewer, respected as the leading African American physician in town, was an early activist working to end segregation in a city steadfastly resistant to change. As the leading member of the local National Association for the Advancement of Colored People (NAACP), he was hated by much of white Columbus.

On February 4, 1956, from his second-story office on First Avenue, Brewer saw a black man, Sylvester Henderson, arrested by a white policeman with, he thought, excessive force. A nightstick was broken over his head. Determined to fight police brutality, Brewer sought to get corroboration of the attack from Luico Flowers, the proprietor of the F&B department store downstairs who had also witnessed the arrest. Entering Flowers's store, Brewer insisted that he give testimony on the beating. Flowers reported this to the police as a threat. Brewer continued to seek Flowers's cooperation and called on him again on the 18th. Flowers shot and killed him there in his store. The grand jury refused to indict Flowers, who claimed he shot in self-defense.

In 1956, the civil rights movement was still in its infancy. Billy Winn, then a senior in high school, says, to his chagrin, that the Brewer killing scarcely made a dent in his memory, despite the fact that his father, a physician, had maintained a proper professional relationship with Dr. Brewer. Billy had been too busy celebrating scoring twenty-five points for his white high school's basketball team to notice.

Outside Columbus, when Brewer's murder is discussed, it is in the context of the fledgling civil rights movement and the physician's bold pioneering efforts locally. But here in Columbus, when local black people—with long memories—speak of it, they tell of a century-long chain of killings of black men by white men. It was only the details that made this one different. If a social scientist would call Brewer's death a political assassination and T. Z. Cotton's a lynching, people in the projects in Columbus would tell you that it doesn't make much difference. They're both dead.

IN 1977, THERE was another death in Columbus. This time, unlike the death of Brewer, no public political issue was involved. It was different too from the death of Cleo Land. This time, there was no question about whether or not it had been a murder or that the victim was deliberately attacked, with a horrible result. The dead person was Carol Jeannine Galloway.

A young white woman of twenty-three, Jeannine was leaving her house to drive to meet a friend. When her car did not leave the driveway, her mother stepped outside, wondering why. Not seeing Jeannine, and noticing that the door to the driver's seat was open, Hettie Galloway called out to her daughter. From the utility room of the carport, Jeannine called to her, with apparent calm, saying that she was looking for something and that her mother should go back in the house.

Worried and flustered, Mrs. Galloway tried to call a neighbor—and misdialed. Then, hearing the car start up, she went out, saw Jeannine at the wheel with a man in a red shirt next to her, and called to Jeannine to stop. Her daughter called out that she would be right back—and drove off. William Anthony Brooks, a twenty-two-year-old black man, was holding a gun against her side. He directed her to drive to a remote spot, ordered her through deep woods into a remote low-lying spot two hundred yards behind a school, forced her to strip, and raped her.

In the dread calm after his ejaculation, Brooks was momentarily inert. Galloway got up, dressed—and then, apparently, her carefully maintained restraint gave way. She screamed, and Brooks, panicking too, shot her in the neck and ran away.* During the next two hours, Jeannine slowly bled to death. Whether during that time she regained consciousness is not known.

Until Jeannine's body was found, all of Columbus knew only of the abduction, but her guessed-at fate was on many minds. When the body was discovered, rape was quickly confirmed. Rage swung to relief in the white community when Morris Comer, who was black, was arrested and identified by Hettie Galloway as the man in the car with her daughter; confusion when Comer established his innocence; and relief once more when someone in Atlanta, seeing the picture drawn from the descriptions given by people who had seen Brooks leaving Columbus, notified the police. Brooks had, with difficulty, managed to persuade someone to give him a lift. William Anthony Brooks was brought back to Columbus's gaunt old red brick jail to await trial.

The trial took place in the new eight-story glass and stone

---

*Years later Gloria Crew, a juror in the second murder trial, hypothesized that Jeannine had kept her cool until dressed and then let loose with a scream. William then panicked and shot her.

Government Center in Columbus, which, devoid of greenery, rises, a tombstone to justice, in place of the park and the old 1896 courthouse. When District Attorney E. Mullins Whisnant of the Chattahoochee Judicial District—in Georgia, the districts, embracing several of the 159 counties, are named for rivers—took the elevator to the orange and brown courtroom, he was fully confident of winning his case. The horror of the Galloway case had spread from Columbus to the rest of the state; there had been a great deal of publicity. Given the statewide interest, the Brooks trial was the first to be televised in Georgia.

As the proceedings got underway with the selection of a jury, the court-appointed defense lawyers, Patrick J. Araguel, Jr., and his partner, Jerry D. Sanders, did challenge the underrepresentation of black citizens in the jury pool—there were only six of 180—but the judge immediately ruled against them. With an all-white jury selected, the trial began. William Brooks had confessed to the police, claiming the shooting was an accident.

All the descriptions of the suspicious man seeking a ride out of town suggested that he was indeed the murderer. Hettie Galloway was Whisnant's first witness. In a voice no less telling for its near inaudibility, she recounted her daughter Jeannine's departure that morning. The man in the car with her had on a red shirt. Was that man in the courtroom? the district attorney asked. "That's him right there."[4]

Cross-examining Mrs. Galloway, Defense Attorney Araguel had her confirm that on July 20, 1977, she had "observed a lineup at the Police Department of several black males" and had picked out one of them. "I said," she told the lawyer, "there was one that looked more like him than any, but it didn't look like him [Brooks]." Mrs. Galloway had picked out Morris Comer; William Brooks, in the courtroom, had not been in the lineup. Araguel then had Morris Comer brought into the courtroom. "Is this the man you said looked like the man that was in the car with your daughter?" he asked. "Well, the best I can remember that looks like him," she replied.[5]

Other than to expose Mrs. Galloway's version of the old "they

all look alike" perception, Araguel had made little headway
with this cross examination, or any other, that first day of the
trial. When, the next afternoon, he presented witnesses for the
defense, he had no more luck. The first person that he called
was Gwendolyn Brooks Thomas, a sister two years older than
William. She was living in an Atlanta suburb when her brother
sought refuge in the city and testified that she had encouraged
him to cooperate with a Columbus police officer who called on
her when he warned of "a bunch of rednecks, and a bunch of
drunken police officers in Atlanta in a manhunt for my brother."[6]

Brooks's lawyer had seen to it that the jurors knew that she
had been tricked into cooperation, but little more. As
Gwendolyn Thomas tried to respond to Araguel's questions
about her brother's behavior, character, and history, a battery of
objections by the district attorney destroyed her narrative.
Araguel then got an unsophisticated fingerprint technician to
cast some doubt on the attribution to Brooks of a print said to
have been taken from Jeannine Galloway's car. Neither testimony was enough to dent Whisnant's powerfully told story of the
abduction, rape, and murder.

When court reconvened the next morning, Araguel argued
that the police, under great pressure to come up with a killer,
had reached too quickly to Brooks, who confessed only when
they threatened to lock up his family. He went on to point out
that none of the witnesses who said they saw William at crucial
moments on that day had been able to make a definitive identification of him. He urged the jurors not to convict a man on cir-
cumstantial evidence.

The prosecutor then, at greater length, reviewed the evidence
against Brooks, told the jurors that a "reasonable doubt, ladies
and gentlemen, is not a fanciful doubt," and stressed that their
responsibility was "the discovery of the truth."[7] It took the jury
an hour and thirty-six minutes to find William Brooks guilty of
capital murder.

After an hour and a half break for lunch, the jurors were back to perform their second duty, making the decision whether William Brooks should live or die. They were to hear arguments on Brooks's sentence. Under the law, if there were sufficient aggravating circumstances, they should sentence him to die; if these were outweighed by sufficient mitigating circumstances, he should, instead, spend the rest of his life in jail.

Araguel left the matter of sparing Brooks's life to his associate, Jerry Sanders, who called William's mother to the stand. She told how her husband, William's father, whom she later divorced, "mistreated the family," adding that "William always felt that he wasn't loved." At this point, Whisnant jumped in with an objection: "she couldn't know how he felt." The judge sustained this objection, the first of many as the prosecutor successfully fractured the story of deprivation that Sanders tried to elicit. As William's mother was telling how, when she was at work, he was "constantly beaten" by her husband, Whisnant objected, saying she could not know that if she were not there.[8]

Gwendolyn Brooks Thomas and one of William's other sisters, Beverly Brooks, also testified. As Gwendolyn began to pour out the tale of William's beatings, being locked up, not being allowed to go to school, of her inability to make her mother, off at work, understand what was happening, of William's having to lie to his mother out of fear of the stepfather, Whisnant mocked it all: "Your honor, she's making a speech." The judge responded: "I can't see where that's helpful to this jury anyway, Mr. Sanders, as to whether his mother inquired as to why they were not in school."[9] Befuddled, the defense attorney's efforts to show the increments of psychological damage to Brooks dissipated.

In cross examination, Whisnant shrewdly steered Gwendolyn Brooks's testimony away from the defense's point by encouraging confusion over whether it was a father or stepfather who left the family, whether the children were this age or that, in order to trivialize a young black woman's testimony. He deflected the main thrust of the sister's account of William's horrendous childhood, leaving the impression that nothing of this treatment of a juvenile had anything to do with William having once, as a teenager, been sent to jail. The jury was left with only a stereo-typical picture of a tattered black family whose troubles were irrelevant to the crime that had been committed.

The witnesses excused, Mullins Whisnant rose to address the jury in a classic championing of the death penalty: "Punishment has a two-fold purpose . . . to punish the guilty offender . . . to deter others. . . ." The punishment should "fit the crime, and the crime in this case is murder. . . ." For which, in this case, "the only appropriate punishment is death in the electric chair." Not merely execution, but specifically and dramatically, in the elec-tric chair. "Mr. Araguel is going to tell you that there is no proof that the death penalty deters crime, you can't prove it. But, I can tell you this; the last person in Georgia was electrocuted in 1964, and since that date, crime has increased year by year . . . every time the statistics come out, we have an increase in [the] crime rate. We didn't have that when we had capital punish-ment."[10]

Then he turned to the two families involved and stressed that Jeannine Galloway was "a pretty young lady . . . a person of high morals. . . ." The defense attorneys will tell you that "locking him up is enough, don't put death on him, don't make his family go through with that." But think of the Galloway family: "Next week when it's Thanksgiving, and [the Galloway family is] sitting around the table, Carol Jeannine won't be there, and never will be there again." Another person whose grief oddly went unmen-tioned by Whisnant was the man to whom Jeannine was engaged to be married. It served the prosecutor's purpose to stress her vir-ginity; "a beautiful young lady . . . not married . . ." still living "with her mother and father."[11]

Whisnant turned to the punishments he felt this killing demanded, saying, "we don't take this business of asking for the death penalty lightly." In his seven and a half years as dis-trict attorney, "I believe we've only asked for it less than a dozen times." But surely, he suggested, this time it was war-ranted. He described how Brooks, ". . . after he's satisfied his lust . . . turns around and shoots her down like you would a dog, a stray dog . . . and she bled to death, very slowly, drip by drip, drop by drop." He reiterated that there was overwhelming proof of guilt of "a horrible crime."[12]

Could William Brooks be rehabilitated?

> There's no chance that William Anthony Brooks will ever be rehabilitated. . . . His own sisters told you that he was a car thief when he was a young child. And, they talked to you about him being beaten by his stepfather, but they never did say what his stepfather was beating him for, maybe he needed it. There's nothing wrong with whipping a child, some of them you have to whip harder than others. And there's been children who have been abused and beaten, but they don't turn to a life of crime on account of it. Goodness sakes, I got whippings when I was a child . . . my daddy used to beat me, but that doesn't give me an excuse to go out and commit a crime.[13]

Turning to the responsibility on the jurors' shoulders, Whisnant admitted that they would ask: "Can I take somebody's life? Well, the truth of the matter is, you're not taking his life, you're not pulling the switch in the electric chair," and neither are "the police who investigated this case" or the Recorder's Court Judge, who conducted the preliminary hearing, and not "me and my staff . . . the person who is responsible for [taking] his life is William Brooks himself, and if the switch is pulled and he's put to death, he pulled the switch the morning that he was walking along Saint Mary's Road when he put the gun in the back of Carol Jeannine Galloway. . . ."[14]

Brooks, he insisted, "has demonstrated that he's a killer." He would endanger any young prisoner "trying to be rehabilitated so he can go back to his family." And if he escapes? What is more, it "costs . . . thousands of dollars a year to keep a prisoner housed, fed and clothed, and medical care, why should the taxpayers, and that's you folks, all of us . . . have to keep up somebody like William Brooks [for] the rest of his life, when he's done what he's done?"[15]

Whisnant then cited the three wars in his lifetime. Young men have "killed other human beings who were enemies of our country, and when they did a good job of killing them, we decorated them and . . . praised them for it. Well, I say to you that we're in a war again in this country, except it's not a foreign nation, it's against the criminal element in this country. . . ." William Brooks is a "member of the criminal element, and he's our enemy. . . . William Brooks is a cancer on the body of society, and if we're going to save society and save civilization, then we've got to remove them from society."[16]

The Muscogee County district attorney wrapped up his argument by insisting that William Brooks had evil on his mind the morning of the murder; he wasn't "just walking along with a pistol in his pocket, and decided, 'Well, I'll make a hustle,' to use their language." For the first time, Whisnant made explicit the racial point that you, the jurors, are different from them and "their language."[17]

During Whisnant's long, impassioned plea, the defense attorneys raised not one objection. When Sanders rose in William Brooks's behalf and made as his most telling point, in a churchgoing community, the biblical commandment: "Thou shalt not kill," Whisnant promptly objected: "He's standing there saying [to the jurors] that they shall not kill." In response, the judge reminded the defense attorney of the "separation of the powers of the Church and State. . . . This jury must decide this based on what the Georgia law is."[18]

At 2:58 P.M., the jury retired to deliberate whether William Brooks should live or die. In a little less than an hour they found that the "rape, and the offense of murder was outrageously or wantonly vile, horrible and inhuman. . . ." Brooks was to die.[19]

The Columbus newspapers, covering the trial fully, give no indication of what the response to the sentencing was in the

African American community. No doubt it looked to many—perhaps all—that William was guilty of the killing; but guilty or innocent, they wouldn't have expected much from that court-room. Certainly, William's family had not. Gwendolyn Brooks recalls William's attorney telling them at the outset that he "couldn't do anything for them. He only took the case because it was assigned to him."[20] His name began with an "A"; he was at the top of the alphabetical list of available lawyers.

Old racial patterns were holding in Muscogee County. The judge who presided over the trial, who sentenced William Anthony Brooks to die in the electric chair, was the Honorable John H. Land. Perhaps the sins of the fathers should not be recalled, but the older people, telling the young, all knew that the judge was the son of Brewster Land, who, in response to a death, had seen to a death sixty-five years earlier.

7

The Underground Railroad

ILLIAM BROOKS WAS taken back to the grimy red brick Muscogee County Jail in downtown Columbus; his sisters and mother went back home. They knew no way to do anything further, save pray. They were helpless as the months and years of the required appeals process seemed to lead only to William's execution. There was nothing in their knowledge of the world that would give them any handle on the legal system. Luckily for them—and for William—there was someone in Georgia committed to ending the death penalty who had such a grasp. Patsy Morris got on the telephone as she had been doing since 1976.

Harriet Pratt Morris was an unlikely dispatcher for a southern underground railroad. A Yankee patrician—her great-grandfather, Charles Pratt, was a founder of the Standard Oil Company—she was brought up on an estate on Long Island and attended Vassar College. When she graduated, she married John B. Morris, a young Episcopalian priest. Nothing at the time of her marriage foretold recruiting lawyers to prevent executions in Georgia. But when in 1954 her husband was given a church in the South, the Morrises found themselves in the midst of the struggle for civil rights; for Patsy (as everyone called her), fighting the death penalty was part of the unfinished business of that movement. In 1958 they moved to Atlanta, where John Morris headed a denominational effort toward integration.

The Morrises helped organize the Georgia chapter of the American Civil Liberties Union, of which Patsy became half of the staff of two. From behind big, round, dark-rimmed glasses, she began monitoring all death penalty sentences when the Supreme Court reinstated the death penalty in 1976. As *The New York Times* would later put it: "Good-natured but firm, she pressed lawyers in Georgia and elsewhere to accept [appeal] cases without fee."[1]*

Over her protestations—"of course, I'm not a lawyer"— lawyers soon realized that the persuasive woman on the telephone knew her law.[2] And she knew the stops on the railroad, one of which was the Unitarian Universalist All Souls Church in Washington, D.C., where a fledgling lawyer named George Kendall in 1979 attended a meeting on the death penalty. He was seated in a white-sided box pew in the handsome building, a copy of London's St. Martins-in-the-Fields. In the high mahogany pulpit that evening was one of the few Georgians who were defending men on death row. Millard Farmer was recruiting volunteers for work that just three years earlier had not been necessary—saving people from execution.

Farmer—speaking, appropriately, from the pulpit—was as much a preacher of the gospel of anti–capital punishment as he was a colorful courtroom lawyer. A native of Newnan, Georgia, and a maverick, he had given up lucrative family concerns to fight the cases in which eager prosecutors were once again calling for the death penalty. In the wake of the Supreme Court Gregg decision (1976), cases were piling up. The first client lost

*Harriet Morris died of cancer in the spring of 1997.

to the electric chair, John Spenkelink, had recently been executed, and more were likely. That spring, on Florida's death row alone, there were 131 men and one woman.[3]

As any lawyer in the pews knew, the Supreme Court, in 1963, responding to Clarence Gideon's pencil-written appeal, required that lawyers be supplied for indigent defendants in criminal cases. Georgia conformed; its laws call for counsel not only for the defendant's trial but also for the direct appeal to the Georgia Supreme Court after a death sentence is imposed. But there the Gideon protection ends; it does not require that a lawyer represent a prisoner making further appeals.

With no such requirement, Georgia provided no such support. If no lawyer volunteers to represent him, a barely educated man on death row may enter a courtroom to appeal his sentence and face a prosecutor and judge entirely on his own. Earlier, at his trial, he might just as well have been on his own, given the quality of lawyer sometimes appointed. Farmer, ever the exhorter, told of down-on-their-luck local lawyers who needed a job, who appeared in court drunk, who fell asleep at the defendant's side, or who were simply unprepared. When Farmer described one convicted murderer being led, in handcuffs, into a hearing to appeal his death sentence without an attorney, George Kendall, six months out of Antioch Law School, turned to the woman sitting in the pew with him: "I don't believe this."

As Farmer closed his powerful description of the conditions facing men sentenced to death, he pointed up the long aisle to a man standing near the door, and introduced David Kendall,* who had been the lead lawyer on Spenkelink's case. Kendall was practicing law now in Washington, and, Farmer explained, he was willing to handle local recruiting of lawyers to take such cases.

George Kendall (no relation) took note. A day or two later, he called David Kendall and they sat down over a cup of coffee. After a good talk about the difficulties of death penalty work—and the emotional drain involved—George offered his services.

*Famous now as President Clinton's lawyer.

He expected he might be asked to scurry out to the airport to rush a petition to the Supreme Court or a brief to a seasoned lawyer. But no such gentle apprenticeship was in the offing.

The underground railroad rolled into the station; Patsy Morris, alerted, made her first telephone call to George Kendall the morning after his enlistment. She introduced herself and said: "I hear you'll take the Thomas case."[4] Kendall gulped. Scarcely out of the classroom, he had a death penalty case on his hands.

George Kendall told me about all of this many years later as we sat in a noisy coffeeshop around the corner from his Hudson Street office in New York City. Kendall now does death penalty work for the NAACP Legal Defense and Educational Fund. Married to another criminal defense lawyer, and hopelessly intent on his new role as a father, he has not let up. Not long ago, his wife asked him if he really wanted to spend the rest of his life in this line of work and he began to wonder. But when she went to court one day and heard him argue a death penalty case, she quietly told him he was doing what he had to do.

Donald Thomas had been convicted of murder, sentenced to the electric chair, and had his sentence upheld by the Georgia Supreme Court. If constitutional error had marred the proceedings, the United States Supreme Court might order a new trial. Needed was a petition for a writ of certiorari, a formal appeal for the Court to intervene.

In law school, Kendall had been all through the drill of how cases were brought to the Supreme Court, but it is one thing to read about how it's done for an upcoming class and another to actually write to that august Court in a life or death matter. He talked the case over with Russ Cannan, a partner in a law firm set up by recent graduates of the Antioch Law School where he worked. They quickly agreed that they needed "another hand on the oar."[5] Cannan had handled cases with Stephen Bright, who had been in the Public Defender's Office, and told Kendall that Bright might be his oarsman.

Kendall called Bright, asking for help. Bright said sure, and put in an intense weekend in the Justice Department's library boning up on Georgia law—and every applicable point within it that they could raise in Thomas's favor. Meanwhile, Kendall called Patsy Morris and asked her to send them the complete record of the case. Since it was a capital case, they expected a great mass of material—"when will the Ryder truck pull up?" they wondered. When the record arrived, it was one lean envelope.[6]

Thomas had been without a lawyer at his pretrial hearing; he had a court-appointed lawyer for his trial and for the subsequent mandatory appeal to the supreme court of Georgia. Now there was no one to represent him in appeals to the federal courts. The very thinness of the record of Thomas's story from crime to conviction underscored the importance of Kendall, Cannan, and Bright's task. Working intensely, the three lawyers identified constitutional errors in the Thomas case, wrote the petition, and, a bit nervously, filed it. It was a heady moment only a month later when they received a copy of the Supreme Court's brief order to the Georgia Supreme Court that it review its decision.

Without hearing any argument on what the United States Supreme Court had detected as a clear constitutional error, the state court simply reaffirmed its earlier decision that Thomas should be executed. Sensing an affront to the Supreme Court, Kendall and Bright again asked the justices to intervene. They were greatly disappointed when, this time, the Supreme Court let the Georgia court's decision stand.

At this point, Kendall and Cannan could have gone back to their District of Columbia law firm full time while Bright continued to direct his student volunteers. And Donald Thomas could have been executed. The lawyers had done what they knew how to do, what they could do without "screwing up," the "reading and writing" they had learned in law school. To try to rescue Thomas in the Georgia court was a different ball game. I asked Kendall why they stepped up to bat. Swirling the ice in his Coke, Kendall mused: "The thought of staying with that case and doing all that traveling . . . had we known where all this would lead. . . ." His voice trailed off, then he added: "One of the great things about life is that you don't know."[7]

But what they did know was that if they didn't take the Thomas case, no one would. "As we began to see the big picture, we knew that there was no way that we were going to turn this case over to someone else." There was no someone else. "So we sort of back-ended into it." They called Patsy Morris and told her they would be down to Atlanta to take it on.

Over the course not only of the Thomas case but all the other cases they took across the state, Kendall, a New Englander, learned, dimly at first, something about the South. On one case he walked into the Butts County Courthouse and asked the clerk of the court, David Ridgeway (who turned out to be not a bad guy at all), "David, what's the balcony for?"[8]

Kendall and Bright were in those days simply strangers in a foreign land, coming to realize just how well death penalty defendants were being served under the supposedly fair procedures that the Supreme Court justices had stipulated when they reinstated capital punishment. And how mysteriously. Seven years later, in 1986, having won a second sentencing trial for Donny Thomas, and waiting for it to be scheduled, they received word that the judge, without Thomas or his lawyers present, signed an order sentencing him to life in prison.

IN 1979, THE same year she recruited Bright and Kendall for the Thomas case, Patsy Morris had the William Brooks case on her hands. The Georgia Supreme Court had let stand Judge Land's death sentence for William Anthony Brooks. With no one in Muscogee County prepared to appeal the ruling, Morris obtained the pro bono services of a midwestern corporate lawyer who took on filing a petition with the Supreme Court in Brooks's behalf. It worked; the Court ordered the Georgia Supreme Court to reconsider the sentence. In 1980, the Georgia justices did so—and reinstated Brook's death sentence.

By then, the lawyer was committed to work for his corporate client and declined to continue with the Brooks case. So, Patsy

Morris put in another call to Washington. Bright and Kendall, still living in the capital, agreed once again to submit a petition to the Supreme Court for a Georgian they did not know, William Brooks. This time they were rebuffed. The legal door on another Georgia defendant was closed—and might have stayed closed.

When the two looked at the record, sizable in the case of William Brooks, and saw how it had been handled not only by his appointed trial lawyers but also by the prosecutor and judge, they realized that the work called for was not a ten-minute trip to the Supreme Court Building to deliver a formal brief, but a flight down to Georgia. If they were going to keep William Brooks alive, they had to be, as Kendall put it, their client's biographer. Reaching into their own shallow pockets, they flew to Atlanta, rented a car, drove the one hundred miles to Columbus, and headed for the jail. "Grim" is too weak a word for the Muscogee County Jail; "medieval" is Kendall's word. Entering, they waited in the room designated for lawyers and inmates to meet their client.

William Brooks was brought in by guards to encounter two young, eager white men. Kendall and Bright, for their part, were facing an overweight and clumsy young black man—"Fats" was his nickname in the local newspapers. Rapport was not instant. Brooks recalls being dubious about the two men, whose accents and use of words sounded strange to his ear. For their part, Bright and Kendall didn't know what to make of their new client. Knowing the guards would allow them only a limited amount of time, they tried quickly to draw Brooks out. Skeptical, he fed them a line with his disconcerting stutter. Finally, Stephen Bright leaned forward, stuck his boyish white face into Brooks's black face, and, in a voice closer to one he would have used back in Kentucky, said, "William, they're going to kill you. What you've been telling us is garbage and you know it is. So, cut the bullshit; you've got to trust us—so trust us."[9]

8

William Brooks

WILLIAM BROOKS DID trust his new lawyers "because they were straightforward with me."[1] Haltingly, through his speech impediment, William told Bright and Kendall about himself. The pages on his case and the hundreds of pages of related cases that Bright and Kendall had absorbed could not substitute for knowing a human being named William Brooks. To these lawyers, he was neither a statistic nor a component of a legal procedure they had undertaken to correct. Brooks was their client. It was their job to keep him alive.

After their first conversation with William, Bright and Kendall talked with his mother and three of his sisters, Shirley, Beverly, and Gwendolyn. They were building William Brooks's life story. He was born in 1955 in France to Beatrice Harmon Brooks, whose army sergeant husband, John Brooks, was stationed there. For the crucial first three months of his life, William was kept in the hospital. As an eighth-month baby, he was not expected to live. Later that same year the Brooks family followed the father's orders to Fort Campbell, Kentucky, where William was again hospitalized. In 1957, Sergeant John

Brooks was ordered to Fort Benning, adjacent to Columbus, Georgia. Once more, the family moved.

William as a small child was overweight, and when he began to talk, he stuttered. As a psychologist later concluded, this was related to an early implanted sense of fear. His physical inability to talk freely, to articulate without stuttering, was accompanied by difficulty reading words on a printed page. William recalls only one teacher, a Ms. Ingram, who, in the fifth and sixth grades, helped him with his speech. There was still less guidance at home. At Fort Benning, his father began drinking and William was engulfed in a household steeped in violence.

The story of this violence was told in full only years later when, reluctantly, but to save their brother, William's three sisters testified at his second trial. Shirley said of her parents:

> There were physical fights. They would start out in arguments and when I mean physical fights, I remember one incident where my father had been drinking the weekend; came home; he started arguing with my mother and they got into a fight. And he took one of my mother's high-heeled shoes and physically beat her in the head with it until he saw blood. There was blood all on the floor. She was just about unconscious.
>
> And, then, myself and my two brothers came down to stop it. He threatened us. And we would still physically try to make him stop. My older brother told us to just divert him for a moment. He went outside and got a log and came back with the log and threw it in my father's chest and knocked him out. That was the only way that we could stop him.
>
> We ran down to a neighbor's house, Mrs. Howard, and she took us all to her house; came back and called the ambulance for my mother and the Military Police.

Asked if William was present at this episode, Shirley replied:

> William was always present. We would make the younger children, Gwen, Marvin and William, stay upstairs so they

wouldn't witness all of this. But they were always downstairs screaming and hollering for my father to stop. We would have to comfort them and tell them that everything would be all right, that my father wasn't going to hurt my mother. And it just took a long time to keep William calm through all these ordeals."[2]

For a long time, William's mother, a small woman who weighed only about one hundred pounds, refused to acknowledge these beatings; they were always "accidents" when she got to the emergency room. When William was nine, his parents separated and Beatrice Brooks moved the family into a comfortable house in a Columbus project. Receiving no child support, she worked two jobs—one all day, the other in the evening. Exhausted, she was with the children only when they all got up in the morning and when she was home to make dinner.

In the late 1960s, John Brooks moved out of state and Beatrice divorced him. But things did not get better; she married Allen Gohlson, much younger than she, and brought him into the troubled home. As Gwen, the sister closest in age to William, recalled, "he drank a lot and he always brought other guys around the house. He always made sexual advances to me and my friends. And I just didn't like him."[3]

And apparently Allen Gohlson felt the same about William. "I think he hated him," Gwen reported. Asked: "How did he treat him?" "Well, he beat him with belt buckles, extension cords. It would be nothing for him to just curse him out; slap his head up against the wall. . . . He seemed to really have a thing about William." Once, coming home from a volleyball game, Gwen walked into the project to find "this big crowd of people at the corner of our building. And that big crowd was there because my brother was screaming for his life. . . . As I got to my front steps, my girl friend sort of informed me that my brother had been screaming like that for over thirty minutes and to please make that man stop."[4]

Gwen went into the house and up the stairs: "I had to beat

down his bedroom door to make him open it. . . ." "Was the door locked?" "Yes, it was. And I finally got that door open. All I could see was my brother laying across a mattress that was on the floor. The room was all torn up. There was blood all over the wall, all over him, and they were just sweating profusely, both of them.

". . . [William] was just begging me to please make him stop."

"Were you able to?" Bright asked her on the witness stand.

"Well, I tussled with him [Gohlson] a little bit and he sort of overruled me at that time and told me that if I didn't want the same thing that I'd better get out of there and leave him alone; it was none of my business. And he somehow shoved me out of the door and locked it again. Then . . . he took it out on William." Mocking her as she left, Gohlson asked William, " 'Do you think she could save you?' . . . And he went back to beating William."[5]

Gwen ran for help. She looked for her older brother on the basketball court; he wasn't there. She told everyone she saw to look for him, and then went back home. "Allen was gone and William was just laying there helpless." She called her grandmother, who in turn called the boy's mother. "And, then, my grandmother came over shortly, and by that time, all my other brothers and sisters started coming home and we basically took care of William until some adult could get there."[6]

The biography of William Brooks was getting stouter—and sadder. There was no way that the two lawyers were going to let so damaged a person suffer the final damage of deliberate death. As there had been no relief from either Supreme Court, Georgia's or the United States's, the two lawyers turned now to the local courts, and discovered just how local these courts could be. (One judge, in his chambers, early in Kendall's quest, told him that he would pass along so weighty a request to the court above him: The "good citizens . . . had elected him to handle their divorces, not deal with constitutional issues.")[7]

To spare Brooks's life, the lawyers needed to obtain habeas corpus relief—literally, the bringing of the body from a place of incarceration and into a courtroom. Brooks, they contended, was due another hearing in open court; in other words, a new trial. Since William Brooks was not in Muscogee County but in Butts County, the home of the Jackson Diagnostic Center and death row, Kendall and Bright got ready for a trip to the county court-house in Jackson, the county seat, to appear before Judge Alex Crumbley.

For thirty days they concentrated on a brief, determined that it would be letter-perfect, and contacted and arranged for three expert witnesses who would appear with them. The day of the hearing, the lawyers and the witnesses—one was William Bowers, distinguished for his work on the factor of race in the composition of jury pools, who had flown to Atlanta from Boston—drove to Jackson to appear before Judge Crumbley. Crumbley, not noted for granting habeas relief, was once a pub-lic defender and thought to have "some problems with the death penalty"; conceivably, he was persuadable.[8] (The judge was troubled by the Jerome Bowden case, still under appeal. Bowden was a retarded young man sentenced to death in Muscogee County. When, later, he was permitted to take an IQ test to see if he was qualified to be executed, he barely "passed,"—he told everybody wistfully that he had tried so hard to do well. He was executed in 1984. Elected to the state legis-lature in 1986, Crumbley was instrumental in getting through the nation's first bill sparing retarded persons from the death penalty. He was not reelected.)

As Bowers, whose reputation Judge Crumbley must have been aware of, testified, Kendall recalls "snickering from the bench." Not only did Judge Crumbley not grant habeas corpus relief, but his mocking behavior, odd in light of his sympathetic attention to Bowden, was an eye opener for Bright and Kendall. There were so many hurdles and the Brooks case was, after all, only their second death penalty case. "We were just babes in the woods. We had no idea how much work taking on cases after the person had been convicted would be."[9]

"It is hard for the lay person to understand, but complying to the absolute letter of the rules is essential." To illustrate,

Kendall tells me of the first man executed in post-Gregg Georgia. He and a woman, in separate trials but with jurors picked from the same pool, were convicted of the murder of her husband. At some point, her lawyer filed, on time, the objection that blacks and women were underrepresented in the jury pool. His lawyer, as the deadline for appeal arrived and passed, failed to do so. Neither defendant got relief from the state court system, but a three-judge panel of the federal 11th Circuit granted her relief, citing the Fourteenth Amendment's equal protection clause. No court ever reviewed his identical claim, because his lawyer had not raised it on time. "She lives, he dies; the kicker [is] . . . if you switch the lawyers, she dies, he lives." As Kendall sees it, "the only person in the system who has to know any law is the defense lawyer. The judge and prosecutor can walk all over the Constitution and if the defense doesn't object, it doesn't matter. The system doesn't care."[10]

In the death penalty business there was no room for error and, for Kendall and Bright, no dropping out: "We were in for the long haul." The next stop for the Brooks case was the Georgia Supreme Court, once Crumbley, in the Superior Court, had denied relief at that level. Once again, that court refused to save Brooks and another petition to the United States Supreme Court was turned down. On December 22, 1982, Judge Land set January 13, 1983, as the date for the Brooks execution. William Brooks, on death row, waited.

Time was short. Kendall and Bright, following the rigid rule book, defeated in their attempt to achieve habeas corpus relief using the state court route that led unsuccessfully to the U.S. Supreme Court, now turned to the federal courts. Brooks was in Jackson, in Butts County, in the jurisdiction of the United States District Court for the Middle District of Georgia—and Judge J. Robert Elliot. They knew exactly what their prospects were. The officer who in 1968, during the Vietnam War, commanded the detachment of troops who slaughtered villagers at My Lai, Lieutenant William Calley (who now runs a jewelry store in Columbus), is the only defendant to whom Judge Elliot had ever granted habeas corpus relief. On January 11, 1983, after wait-ing to the last moment, he flatly denied William Brooks such relief.

The next day, January 12, William was taken from his cell on death row and put in the room adjacent to the electric chair. That same day, Stephen Bright walked down Forsyth Street to the federal courthouse to be sure a message had reached the 11th Circuit Court of Appeals. Bright had already filed an appeal, fearing that Elliot would delay his rejection of Brooks's petition for habeas corpus relief until after his execution—in order to ensure it. Eighteen hours before Brooks was scheduled to die, the three judges issued a stay, pending a decision on whether he should have a new trial. Having been with William on his death-watch, his mother and sisters, fearing the worst, were driving to the nearby shelter for deathwatch families run by a private group, when they heard of the stay on the car radio. William Brooks was still alive.

Later that year—in April—the stay still in effect, Bright and Kendall argued for a new trial before a three-judge panel of the 11th Circuit Court. In September, the judges set aside William's death penalty on the grounds that District Attorney Mullins Whisnant's plea to the jury to call for the death penalty had been improper because "the prosecutor played upon the fears and prejudices of the jurors. . . ."[11] This was but one of the judges' objections to his conduct, which was, as Kendall characterized it, a "cookbook of improper arguments."[12] The most pungent was Whisnant's telling the jurors that if they did not impose the death sentence, Brooks would walk out of jail and into their neighborhoods. The three-judge panel ordered a new sentencing trial.

Now it was the state of Georgia's turn to appeal. It called on the full 11th Circuit Court to reverse the three-judge panel's order and allow Brooks to die. They were to be disappointed. The full twelve-member Appeals Court paradoxically concluded in 1985 that it was not the prosecutor who had been in error, but Judge Land. His "instructions as to intent and malice may have confused the jury as to the proper burden of proof."[13] The court, en banc, concluded that a new trial should be held to determine both guilt and, if necessary, the sentence.

The state now turned to the United States Supreme Court, which in 1986 ordered the 11th Circuit Court to reconsider. The judges did so, and, in 1987, stuck by their guns. The state once again appealed to the Supreme Court; this time the justices allowed the 11th Circuit Court's ruling to stand. There was to be a new trial of William Anthony Brooks for the murder of Jeannine Galloway.

DURING THE LONG years of the Brooks case, Stephen Bright had taken a new job. (His advice to law students worried about competition for jobs is to do what he did: take a job no one else wants.) The Thomas and Brooks cases had persuaded him there was no escape from Georgia; commuting wouldn't do it. In August 1982, he left the program in Washington that placed local law students in local criminal trial work and took over the ailing Southern Prisoners Defense Committee. Bright closed its two offices in New Orleans and Nashville, and opened a new one in Atlanta, small quarters downtown in the Healy Building.

As they were loading up a rented van for Steve's move, his lawyer friend Bob Morin said, "You're not going by yourself." Morin, knowing about Bright's health and his propensity for working himself close to the bone, then added, "I'm not going forever, but I'm coming down with you for the move south." Morin, a distinguished defense attorney in his own right and now a judge on the Washington, D.C., Superior Court, stayed a year. George Kendall came down twice that first fall to help; at the end of the second visit, Bright said to him, "Look, I don't have any money, you can see that, but Patsy Morris has raised $15,000. We just need more people in this business. Please think about taking the job."[14]

There were—and are—others in the business. A small network of criminal defense lawyers willing to handle death penalty cases, taking on sentenced clients, exists across the country.

And the lawyers all know one another. The Bright shop quickly became one of the most bustling of those committed to the enterprise. A parade of able lawyers has worked there. Russ Cannan left Washington on a leave of absence and he too was there that first year. When he and Morin went back to Washington, Steve turned to Palmer Singleton, whom he knew slightly. Singleton offered to come for six months; he stayed for six years.

Not a few lawyers now doing capital punishment work got their start with Bright. Clive Stafford Smith at Columbia Law School, who, as an Englishman, believes that many things about America are not just perverse but downright silly, offered to come down to see something truly ridiculous. Steve told him there was no money, but Stafford Smith put together $12,000 and came on his own. He now does death penalty work in Louisiana. The parade of interns began; Bryan Stevenson, down from the Harvard Law School, got the experience in death penalty work that he was to pursue in Alabama. So too did Robert McGlasson in Texas, Ruth Friedman in Alabama, and Carla Friend in Georgia. Ruth Friedman was there during a law school summer prior to joining the group with degree in hand.

Bright was the shop foreman. He put in grueling hours, so everyone else did too, first in the Healy Building in downtown Atlanta and then at the present office at 83 Poplar Street. George Kendall has always been one of the pack. After several trips to Georgia from Washington on the Brooks case, he stopped commuting. He took a job at the American Civil Liberties Union of Georgia, and was paid the $15,000 that Patsy Morris had amassed, and was able, from around the corner, to go on working on death penalty cases with Steve Bright.

As far as anyone could tell, Bright subsisted on peanut butter—sometimes it was the menu for all three meals of the day. Originally, Bright lived in a grim one-room apartment while Morin's place in a basement was labeled "the Cave." When Kendall moved to Atlanta, the two men bought a house on which the mortgage payments were lower than rent. The house, in which Bright still lives, is a frame cottage typical of many on quiet tree-lined streets in southern cities, with a porch in front and a square, shaded yard out back. On the right, room behind room, was the larger half; parallel, on the left, a second apartment.

The two close friends not only continued with the Brooks case but saw it as part of a larger battle. By appealing the death sentences—still few in number compared with what was to come—they were convinced that they could demonstrate that the fairness promised in legislation undergirding the death penalty could not be achieved. In that way, they would bring about its demise.

If Bright and Kendall were concentrating on one case when another arose, they would turn to friends elsewhere in the country to take it. With few states yet ready actively to pursue the death penalty, help could be found. Bright and Kendall would mount an offensive to prove that every carefully constructed legal structure to ensure the fairness Furman had demanded was actually a dodge concealing unfairness. With astonishing optimism, they set out to slay the dragon.

The dragon was not to be slain. If, indeed, there had ever been a chance in that era that it might be, it was lost on April 22, 1987, when the Supreme Court spoke in a case brought by the NAACP Legal Defense and Educational Fund—once again, a Georgia case. Warren McCleskey was one of four black men holding up a store in Atlanta. A white police officer, responding to a silent alarm, confronted the thieves and was shot and killed. One of the bullets that killed him matched those fired from McCleskey's gun and he was convicted of murder and sentenced to death.

The grounds for McCleskey's habeas corpus appeal to the Supreme Court was a remarkably thorough study of the place race played in Georgia prosecutions, directed by David Baldus. A professor of law at the University of Iowa, Baldus, along with his colleague in statistics at Iowa, George Woodworth, and Charles Pulaski, professor of law at Arizona State University, conducted a study of more than 2,484 murder cases in Georgia in the 1970s. They showed that those accused of killing a white person were far more likely to receive the death penalty (11 percent of the cases) than those charged with killing a black person (1 percent of the cases). The study also showed the percentage of cases in which the sentence was death:

black defendant and white victim,	22%
white defendant and white victim,	8%
black defendant and black victim,	1%
white defendant and black victim,	3%

In addition, prosecutors asked for the death penalty in 70 percent of cases where the defendant was black and the victim white; 32 percent of cases with white defendants and white victims; 15 percent of cases with black defendants and black victims; and 19 percent of cases with white defendants and black victims. Baldus, using the most sophisticated statistical analysis, applied 230 variables to the data, none of which demonstrated other than that black defendants who kill white victims have the greatest likelihood of receiving the death penalty.[15]

None of these statistics were startling to anyone acquainted with the history of race relations in the South, but the specificity of the voluminous, exhaustively researched study made the facts plain and difficult to refute. Empirically, it showed that post-Furman statutes, which had promised to remove death from the death equation, were failing just as pre-Furman ones had. The justices of the Supreme Court did not refute the facts or the conclusion; they acknowledged them to be valid even as they ignored them and confirmed McCleskey's death sentence. After further appeals, he died in the electric chair in September 1991.

The McCleskey case marked the close of the remarkable commitment to racial justice by the justices of the United States Supreme Court maintained since they ended legal segregation in 1954. In the Brown against the Board of Education decision, the court, speaking unanimously, made specific use of the work of the Swedish sociologist Gunnar Myrdal, who in his *American*

Dilemma (1944) contended that black children were damaged psychologically by having to attend separate schools.

In McCleskey, a very different Supreme Court had before it statistically reliable evidence of racial discrimination. The Baldus study showed that the concept of color-blind justice, so proudly championed in a nation wearied of the still tough job of achieving racial justice, was a myth. But despite the Baldus numbers, Justice Lewis Powell held that it could not be shown that in this specific case race played a part. Chief Justice William Rehnquist, and Justices Byron White, Sandra Day O'Connor, and Antonin Scalia, agreed.

Without "far stronger proof," statistical evidence was not relevant to this claim; there was not statistical evidence of racial discrimination in the seating of the juries that convicted and sentenced McCleskey. And, the opinion held, there was the necessity of maintaining the legitimate discretion of prosecutors. Neither the Fourteenth Amendment nor the Eighth had been violated, the Court concluded.

Most chilling of all was this frank conclusion: "McCleskey's claim, taken to its logical conclusion, throws into serious question the principles that underlie the entire criminal justice system."[16] Hundreds of other convicts would be able to claim they were the victims of the same inequity, and in the future, prosecutors would be held to a concept of equal justice. Indeed, lower federal appeals courts had found constitutional errors in a great many death penalty convictions; there might come to be a flood of these reversals, if capital punishment were not left essentially to the state courts.

In a brilliant dissent—one of his most eloquent—Justice William Brennan called this "fear of too much justice."[17] Dissenting as well were Justice Thurgood Marshall, a longtime death penalty foe, who knew all too well what Baldus was telling his fellow justices, and Justices Harry Blackmun and John Paul Stevens, both of whom were still conscious of racial inequities and were becoming more uneasy about capital punishment.

In an interview after his retirement, Justice Powell said that the McCleskey decision was the decision that he most regretted. Had he reached that judgment when it mattered, not only would Warren McCleskey still be alive, but successful appeals of black defendants would have been made far more likely and the power of prosecutors unilaterally to decide which defendants deserved the death penalty put in question. But Powell had not reached that judgment, and now there seemed to be no firm federal collar on how the state criminal justice system worked.

IT WAS IN this legal atmosphere that William Brooks's case proceeded. In 1987, the Muscogee County Grand Jury once again indicted William Anthony Brooks for murder. If the passion of the white community in the immediate aftermath of the murder of Jeannine Galloway had abated over time, the determination of the frustrated prosecutors of Muscogee County to avenge her murder had increased. They were deeply resentful of the do-gooder aliens who had taken up William Brooks's cause. Mullins Whisnant was no longer the district attorney; he had become a Superior Court judge. But he was not far removed from the prosecutorial scene. His assistant, Douglas Pullen, was now district attorney—and determined to finish the job with the execution of William Brooks.

Stephen Bright and George Kendall were equally determined that Brooks should not be killed. To aid in the defense, they brought in two other lawyers: Ruth Friedman, new at the center, and Gary Parker. Parker, tall, handsome, and gregarious, was not an outside agitator. Columbus's leading black lawyer, he likely would have held that rank even if black colleagues had been less scarce than they were. The team was, as Kendall recalls, "a very collegial group," but Bright "was clearly the lead lawyer."[18] William Brooks, who back in 1980 would have been without counsel, was now represented by an impressive array of legal talent.

Bright piled one motion after another in an ingenious effort to keep Brooks alive. The frustrated Muscogee County prosecutors were equally determined to achieve the execution they were sure they had won so long ago. Bright and Kendall's attempt to have Brooks's sentence vacated on the grounds of underrepresentation of African Americans on the jury was unsuccessful. But against a motion charging prosecutorial misconduct, Pullen responded that he asked for the death penalty when there were aggravating circumstances to the crime, when the defendant had a previous criminal record, and when the victim's family requested it.

It was clear that the district attorney had consulted the Galloways, but, in other cases, had he asked the victim's families? Three of the women at the center, Mary Eastland, Ruth Friedman, and Gay Nease, set out to interview members of these families. Nease, a widow with three children, and a recent graduate of the West Virginia Law School, had come to the center as a volunteer. She soon proved to be an expert investigator; not much would escape the scrutiny of these three. They obtained a court order and went through the files of homicide prosecutions in Muscogee County to identify cases where the victims were black. They then called on the families and found that they had not been talked to by Pullen. Ruth recalls one woman who had had two sons murdered. She received no cooperation from the district attorney's office, had been ejected from the courtroom when she screamed out in protest, and learned only on the television news that the killer of one of her sons had pleaded guilty and received a lesser sentence.[19] That racism infected the criminal justice system in the county seemed clear, but this too was held by the judge not to be prosecutorial misconduct.

One motion, for which Ruth Friedman wrote the brief, was granted: the Georgia Supreme Court established the right of an indigent defendant to request the judge to authorize the use of state funds to bring in necessary expert witnesses without revealing to the prosecution what the trial strategy would be. (The prosecution already had the equivalent right.) This meant not only that expert witnesses such as social workers could be obtained to testify in Brooks's behalf, but that a precedent was set that has since proved valuable in litigation in other states.

For Friedman, one of the reasons she prefers capital defense work is the intellectual challenge. Unlike so much other legal work, the lawyer in death penalty cases must "invent and create" the law. There is little established law directly addressing the inequities facing defendants who are poor. But she by no means sees the work of establishing such general propositions as superior in importance to the job at hand, representing the defendant. She bristles at being called a "death penalty lawyer," as prosecutors often do; like the others at the center, she represents not a cause but a client.[20]

The flurry of motions by Bright, moving up to higher courts and back again, proved increasingly exasperating to District Attorney Pullen. The coziness of the legal establishment in Muscogee County was, in fact, making it difficult for the Superior Court of the Chattahoochee District to come up with a judge for the new trial. Although Judge Land had been cleared of formal charges, his membership in a White Citizens' Council back in the days of its battle against the civil rights movement made him vulnerable to an appeal, should he have retried the case. Having been the original prosecutor, Judge Whisnant recused himself, and so, before the case began, did the court's third judge. Judge Hugh Lawson of the Oconee Judicial District agreed to take the case. It was he who ruled in all the pretrial motions; now he would try Brooks for murder.

Bright, on the grounds that there had been prejudicial publicity in Columbus, was granted a change in locale for the new trial. A county with roughly the same white to black demographic balance needed to be found. A good many were proposed; for example, relatively liberal DeKalb County reaching into Atlanta was proposed by Bright; Pullen favored conservative Cobb County north of Atlanta. Neither suited both men. Finally, Morgan County in the Ocmulgee Judicial District was proposed and agreed to. The Brooks trial would be held in the Morgan County seat, Madison, a village fifty miles east of Atlanta in the green fields of east-central Georgia.

Through all this time, what was the hope held out to William

Brooks? If Bright were to succeed, he would not be killed; but the prize if Stephen Bright were to win his case would be life in a Georgia prison. As he awaited his new trial, William Brooks could look back on a dozen years in Georgia's jails. And the prospect of a lifetime more—or worse. Twice, he tells me, he has had to prepare himself for death, "and watch and wait for some-one to kill you."[21]

9

Phillips State Prison

O N A CRISP, clear January morning in 1997, I gaze past the
gleaming razor wire toward the North Georgia mountains
far in the distance. Then I turn to the tower. Calling up
to the guard far above, I shout that I am here to see Tony
Amadeo. He calls down, "Wearing a pager?" I shout back, "No,"
and, electronically, he rolls back the first massive sliding metal
door. Once through, the second waits to open until the first has
slid shut. Stepping through, it is only a short walk into Tony
Amadeo's prison.

Prisons are not all alike; nor, of course, are the experiences
of the prisoners. Back when I first delved into the boxes marked
"Brooks" in the basement of 83 Poplar Street, my attention had
also been drawn to another marked "Amadeo." In it was evidence of a remarkably varied life in prison. Since Bright had
kept him from execution, Tony Amadeo had been serving a life
sentence. I applied for permission to visit him in the Phillips
State Prison in Buford, north of Atlanta, and it was granted.

In the scrupulously clean lobby, four boys, their identical
noses making them unmistakably brothers, are cuffing each

other just in front of me on line as keys, rings, belts—even shoes—are passed around a sensitive metal detector and, as if you're at a rock concert, the back of your hand is stamped. Placing everything but a pocketful of quarters in a locker and putting my stamped hand under an ultraviolet scanner, I walk into a vast room where, row on row, two plastic chairs face two others in a large, windowed room. In white coveralls trimmed in blue, each labeled on the back of the shirt STATE PRISONER, men sit facing relatives and an occasional "special visitor" like me. All around the room, the unused chair next to each prisoner is piled high with plastic snack envelopes, wrapped sandwiches, and soda cans; I knew why I'd been told to bring the quarters—to feed the vending machines. The littlest of the four brothers is wriggling around on the lap of his oldest brother, the one the family has come to see.

As Tony Amadeo walks in, I recognize him from his graduation picture. I have seen it hanging on the wall over Bright's desk at 83 Poplar Street. In the photograph, Tony stands, flanked by Steve and Bill Warner, his other lawyer, the two guests he was permitted to invite, and dressed just as he is today, with the addition of a mortarboard. Amadeo had just delivered the valedictory address, having been graduated, summa cum laude, from Mercer University.

Until the program was halted, faculty members from Mercer's Atlanta campus came to teach at Phillips. Tony remembers the work he did, the papers carefully handwritten on lined paper from the prison store, his dedicated teachers. And he remembers everything else. Few people I have known have as coherent a hold on the memory of their lives as Tony Amadeo does. I catch myself about to quote Samuel Johnson's line about the prospect of hanging concentrating the mind.

DRIVING TO THE prison, I wondered how the conversation with Tony would go. How could I get this man whom I had never met to talk openly about matters that must have been deeply troubling? I needn't have worried. There is no diffidence in Tony

Amadeo. Small rather than imposing, he is open-faced, almost boyish at thirty-nine, and promptly puts a visitor at ease. This openness is, at the same time, a protective shield.

As the morning goes swiftly on and a rich narrative of his life emerges, our conversation cuts back and forth, punctuated by analogies to Procopius, references to Aristotle, quotes from Shakespeare. This display of erudition may, in part, be caused by his knowing that I am an academic. What he does not realize is that I'm just a hardscrabble American historian; he loses me when he gets to ancient philosophy. (There is something to be said for jail; there's time to read. The librarian, he reports, gets him any book he's hungry for.)*

The Amadeo family (their pronunciation is "AM-a-doe," but Tony has given up resisting the Mozartian ring the rest of us give the name) lived in Morgan City, Louisiana, when he was a boy. His only surviving sister recalls an economically secure family "that lived in an almost perfect setting,"[1] a view that Tony only partially shares. Their father was an Italian Catholic, their mother Protestant. Along with a Catholic upbringing, the children were given a good deal of other attention. There is much of his mother and father in Tony still. His mother liked to read poetry to him. His father's efforts at intimacy were more awkward.

Dennis Amadeo was a Marine on Guadalcanal in World War II. Tony uses terms ranging from "shell-shocked" to the currently fashionable "syndrome" to explain his father's manner, his distance from the boy as the two tried to reach each other and his father sought to guide him. When Tony failed in a swimming class, his father threw him into the deep end of the pool with the injunction: "Swim." Tony elected to remember this as

---

*Since my visit, the librarian, discouraged by restrictions placed upon her, has left. Under Commissioner of Corrections Wayne Garner, the emphasis in Georgia's state prisons is on punishment rather than rehabilitation. Libraries and shops teaching trades are being closed, but Tony Amadeo has persuaded the authorities at Phillips State Prison to have a reading group. He and five other inmates meet weekly to discuss a passage of a book that they have all read; presently they are tackling the *Iliad*.

teaching him self-reliance. Time has given his memories of parents a resonance of lost strength.

All of this came to an end at 2:45 A.M. on December 22, 1967. The Amadeos, in the family car, were driving to Tony's grandmother's for Christmas in Texas when a drunken driver, in the wrong lane, hit the car head-on. His mother, father, and one of his sisters were killed; Tony and another sister survived. Desolate and confused, he was packed off to his mother's family in Colorado City, Texas.

The boy's grandmother, perceived by many as "a wonderful person," was, one relative recalls, "racially prejudiced and considers Italians the closest thing to being Black."[2] She agreed to Tony remaining a Catholic, and he found himself dropped off for mass, alone, and picked up when it was over. Worse than this isolation are the reports of an alcoholic uncle who "abused" Tony. (The report of the family member does not say whether the assaults were sexual or in the form of beatings.) Lost from his parents, never really found by the Texas relatives, Tony had to hide in a shell of self. As one wise observer who has known Tony for many years says, Tony never mastered the art of empathy, could never truly see, or, perhaps, dare to see, into the feelings of another person. He certainly failed to do so when, later, he confronted a man named James Turk, Sr.

Despite Tony's undoubted intellect, his high school career came to nothing. After being accused of a theft, reportedly for an escapade with a girl, he was faced with the choice of being charged with a crime or going into the service. In the summer of 1976, at age seventeen, Amadeo followed his father into the Marine Corps.

Tony is small and not a mass of noticeable muscle (he doesn't like exercise much and the one weight machine in the prison is broken). As he tells of the demanding boot camp on Parris Island, I expect to learn of traumatic experiences. Instead, when I ask how he had fared, he replies, "Fine."[3] Amadeo emerged from that strenuous training as one of eight out of eighty-five men ranked as meritorious privates first class and sent to be trained in advanced electronics in a town near Memphis. His schooling went well, too; but when Tony completed the course, with high marks, there were no jobs in the Marine Corps in that field.

Instead, feeling "shafted," he was assigned to the artillery and put to the task of setting fuses—in the dark. If you do it wrong, you blow yourself up. This realization took a toll on his nerves. A buddy suggested speed; that helped, and Amadeo, still only eighteen, began a major venture into drugs—enhanced marijuana, LSD, and amphetamines. Tony's easy sense of humor and confidence yielded to this new compulsion and he quit Camp Lejeune, North Carolina, without leave.

From the hazy account of the days prior to the murder, of James Turk, Sr., in which drugs appear to have played a large part, Amadeo apparently joined up with two other young men he scarcely knew, David Coulter and William Conlogue, with whom he drove aimlessly first to Tennessee, then down into Alabama. There, they committed the first of their murders; it was Coulter who fired the shot that killed the man. Turning that night into Georgia, they slept in Tony's car, a new white Monte Carlo parked along a road west of Atlanta.

Then, early in the morning of September 29, 1977, they headed east on Interstate 20, turned south into Eatonton, and, according to the confession Amadeo signed that night,* "drove around . . . on some back roads looking for a little store to hit. Bill was driving when we spotted an old white man in a brown pickup truck dumping trash in a dumpster. We passed him and turned around to come back." Driving up next to the pickup, "I got out of the back seat with a .22 automatic. I walked up to the truck and I asked for his money. He said he didn't have none. I said yeah, you do." At that point another truck pulled into the

---

*It was transcribed by Dona B. Haislip, Georgia Bureau of Investigation, and signed by Tony B. Amadeo. The conversation apparently was dictated, not written, by Amadeo. The diction is not his now, and was not when he was writing in prison shortly after the murder.

lot: "The man was still in the back of the pickup. Then I shot him. I shot one time. The man grabbed his chest and kind of slid off the right side of the truck to the ground. He turned and yelled for help and started for that other truck. I just ran for our car. . . . We took off."[4]

The evening before our conversation, Tony, lying in his bottom bunk in the nighttime privacy of their cell, had been talking to his "roommate"—Tony's term—in the top bunk. (Tony has a lot of seniority at Phillips.) The cellmate, whose murder is only three years old to Amadeo's twenty, asks, "Can you ever forget?" "No," Tony explains, "you simply have to live with it—every day." And as he tells me how he killed James Turk, his hand closes around an imagined pistol and he recalls a trigger pulled, the shot, a man dead.

As Tony reveals in such graphic detail all—or nearly all—of the story of the murder, I wonder if even he hasn't hidden away from himself some of the horrors of those determinative five minutes of his life. How, I ask, can he think about that man, that man's family? He can't not, is his reply: "I think of them every day." He remembers the family at the trial. Did he dare look at them, I ask. "I turned deliberately to look at them," he replies.

He saw them in 1977 as he sat in the courtroom of the Putnam County Courthouse, commanding its block in the center of Eatonton. With light coming in from the four large, classically proportioned windows on either side wall, he could turn one way to see the Turk family, turn the other to see his grandmother and sister who had come east from Texas.

To represent Amadeo, an indigent defendant, Judge Joseph Duke appointed two lawyers well known professionally and politically, E. Roy Lambert and William A. Prior, Jr. Later, when asked, the lawyers said they considered challenging the make-up of the jury list on the possibility that it might be racially inequitable, but concluded they had no reason to. As they went over the list, they thought they might get a jury that would include "some people that . . . would not be so wanting to give the death penalty."[5] They had no evidence to suggest that the list was not properly constituted. When chosen, the jury was evenly split between black and white Georgians, with a preponderance of women.

The two lawyers not only failed to prevent the jury from finding Tony guilty of murder; they offered no mitigating evidence that might have persuaded the jury to spare Tony's life. The jurors imposed the death penalty. Amadeo's family, in Texas, realizing how desperate the situation was, engaged the services of an Atlanta law firm, which assigned a young associate, William M. Warner, to the case. Warner went immediately to Eatonton to counsel with Tony Amadeo; the visit was the beginning of a long, close relationship with his client whose appeals were to stretch out over thirteen years.

When, in 1979, the Georgia Supreme Court, as it was required to do, reviewed the conviction, the justices did not ask themselves why the lawyers offered no description to the jury of Tony's boyhood life or stressed his excellent early record in the Marines. The fact that his two original lawyers had declined to offer such mitigating evidence when the judge asked if they wanted to do so meant that the constitutional requirements of proper procedure had been met. That, to Warner and Amadeo's dismay, was all these justices needed to know as they affirmed the death sentence.

Awaiting his trial, Amadeo had been held in a cell with other prisoners in the Putnam County Jail, a brick building painted white just off the courthouse square. Although designed to look more like a house than a jail—there is a modest portico at the (unused) front door—a jail it surely was. (It has since been abandoned and a new facility built outside town.) Inside the building the white paint is flaking from the walls, the gray from the doors and bars. To the right on the first floor is the jailer's apartment and the kitchen where, once, the jailer's wife cooked for the prisoners; on the left is one cell for overnighters and a common room which also served as meeting place for lawyers and their prisoner clients.

Up the metal stairs, on the second floor, is a warren of cells, those in the center windowless, with the same double-decker metal cots in each. Graffiti remains as a monument to defiance and, sometimes, as a plea for succor. A well-rendered deer—or is it an elk?—mounts a reclining guard: "Here's your deer meat mother fucker." The penetration is impressive. Above the top bunk in one cell a finely scripted "Jesus" is adorned with a tiny cross; above the bottom bunk of a long-gone occupant is the order to anyone looking in: "Suck my dick."

There is only one solitary cell. Tony Amadeo was moved into it when he was brought back from his conviction and sentencing up at the courthouse. He was held there for the ten months that it took for his appeal to reach, and be rejected by, the Georgia Supreme Court. In the basement of 83 Poplar Street, in a box of things Tony entrusted to Stephen Bright, is his handwritten account of that experience. It matches the story that Tony told me sitting almost knee to knee at Phillips.[6]

"The cell," he wrote, "was small and dark. As I walked through the metal doorway . . . I saw the cell was perhaps seven feet by six feet wide," with a narrow steel cot along one wall; on the other, a toilet, a sink, and, behind a six-foot-high partition, a shower. In the door is a slot through which Tony could be viewed and through which, wordlessly, his food was shoved.

"To prevent the water from splashing out onto the floor I had to fashion a curtain of sorts . . . from the plastic mattress cover on my mattress. The green frayed plastic served its purpose quite well." He writes that the only window was bricked up, barred, and covered with rusting, broken metal mesh. Below was "a rusted and faded white radiator" that banged and put off too much heat for the space. Because of the steam from it and the shower, "a mildew grew on the faded white walls." Higher on the wall over his bunk he found a two-foot-tall cross drawn on the wall by an earlier resident.

The only light was "a 60 watt bulb" set into "a small six-inch space . . . cut into the concrete wall by the door." Over it was a metal flap that could be closed from outside the cell; when it was closed, the darkness was total.

Had I asked how he could stand it, I suppose he would have answered that he had no choice. When I did ask how he kept from going mad, he responded that quite the opposite had happened. His schooling had yielded no poetry he could recite, no history he could force himself to recount. He had only his own story to create out of memories that did not carry with them many niceties.

Because I was classified as a security threat I was not permitted to have anything . . . and I do mean everything! I could not have a radio or television nor could I have magazines, books, pens, paper or anything else." [He was given two sheets, a pillowcase, and a blanket as well as toilet paper, soap (intermittently), and a towel.] Other than this, I had only myself. . . . There was nothing to divide the long days from the even longer nights. . . . For the first few days or weeks I slept as much as was possible. . . .

Slowly the solitude began to weigh in on me. . . . My false courage and bravado . . . began to wane. The folly of my ways began to fill me with depression, despair and loneliness. I sank lower and lower into an ever deepening abyss of stagnant desolation. . . . Ricocheting off the walls . . . were feelings of . . . hatred, despisement and loathing. I hated the world for putting me where I was . . . I despised all mankind for the uncaring torment . . . I felt a bitter loathing for every single person. . . .

The anguish was "a raging fire . . . finally I came to the realization that all the hatred originated from me. The more I hated the more hated I felt. The more suffering I wished upon others the more I myself suffered. I was responsible for being where I was." This is the closest Amadeo came in this Augustinian outpouring to speaking of exactly that external action he was indeed responsible for, the murder of James Turk.

"I lived in a world of mental chaos. Slowly I crept ever closer to the world of total insanity." There was a demon in pursuit;

he named him, oddly, "Lord foul bane." "Please don't be mis-led," he urges his reader, "into thinking that the demon is easi-ly identified and repelled. . . . What power of evil causes evil thoughts to crash in upon the shores of our minds." The fury would not go away, but somehow, Amadeo made it do so. "These thoughts numb . . . by their repetitive occurrence." They could elicit "no more than an occasional shrug."

"To help clear my mind from all the cob-webs of my torment-ed state I began to play mental games with myself. . . . I would take some toilet paper and make a dozen or so pea sized balls. I would wet them with spit and let them dry thereby making them somewhat hard. I would gather these balls in my hand, shake them up, and throw them gently onto the floor. This would scatter them out into a rough circle about two feet in diameter. What I would do then would be to mentally con-nect the balls to form geometric figures . . . triangles, squares, pentagons, hexagons and octagons. I would only look for one specific polygon per toss. . . . After I had found all I could find, I would remove one of the balls and start over.

While Tony was putting his mind in order, another, wholly unrelated mental exercise had been underway. During the sum-mer following Amadeo's trial, a lawyer named Chris Coates was doing archival research in the clerk's office of the Putnam County Courthouse on a case unrelated to Amadeo's—one deal-ing with possible inequities in the registering of voters. Jury lists are one of the records that enable a researcher to compile a demographic profile of a county. As Coates was going through stacks of routine lists of citizens on call as potential jurors in Putnam County, he came upon a memorandum, or rather, a handwritten page of numbers, from District Attorney Joseph Briley to the Putnam County Commissioner of Juries.

Deciphered, the handwritten numbers, divided into cate-gories—black men, black women, white men, white women, and the percentages of each in relation to their representation in the population of the county—made it clear what the commissioner was being instructed to do. Only enough African Americans and women were to be on the list to prevent a successful charge of gender or racial underrepresentation on a jury.

Coates was less surprised by the content of the memorandum than by its having been preserved and put in a file drawer—and found. He surmised that Briley might not only be seeking to circumvent the constitutional requirement forbidding racial or gender discrimination on juries, but also that he was violating proper prosecutorial practice by intruding in the work of the jury commissioner in order to gain juries more amenable to his views.

With this evidence in hand, Coates went into the Federal District Court in Macon in August 1986. Judge Wilbur D. Owens, Jr., a tough judge and one who is a stickler for strict adherence to the Constitution, held the hearing. Owens knew, as any lawyer, including any prosecutor, should, that it was wholly out of order for a prosecutor to instruct those charged with constituting a jury. As R. W. Dennis, clerk of the Superior Court in Putnam County, to whom Briley's instructions had gone, writhed, Owens commented: "Y'all are wasting a lot of time over there in that county trying anybody for a crime." Pressing the point, Coates immediately said, "Your honor . . . We would suggest that the writer of the memo is telling the jury commissioners how to under-represent blacks, but avoid a prima facie case under Fifth Circuit case law."* Said Owens, in response, "Yes sir, looks like it."[7]

The world of people presently working to rid the Georgia system of racial inequity and combat district attorneys not disposed to do so is a small one. Everyone knows everyone else. Not surprisingly, Chris Coates had a conversation with Patsy Morris, the death penalty monitor with the American Civil Liberties Union

---

*The old 5th Circuit Court of Appeals, since replaced in part by the 11th, was the Deep South court that issued many crucial rulings during the civil rights movement.

of Georgia. She was aware that Amadeo's appeal was pending and asked Coates, "Do you know Roy Lambert?" one of Amadeo's original lawyers. He did; they had worked on a case together. "Well, be sure to let Roy know."[8] Morris sensed how crucial this information could be to Amadeo. She was right. If, states Stephen Bright, Chris Coates "hadn't been down there going through those jury lists," Tony Amadeo would be dead.[9]

Coates talked to Amadeo's original lawyer, Roy Lambert, who in turn contacted yet another well-known lawyer, Nelson Jernigan—both of whom were to go on record as saying the issue would certainly have been raised in Amadeo's defense if the memorandum had been at Lambert's disposal. As Lambert put it, "It'd been a great issue if I'd known about it."[10] Jernigan knew it still was. He got a photocopy of the memorandum to William Warner, now Amadeo's lawyer, who took the case to the state courts. When they failed to call for a new trial for Amadeo, Warner turned to the Federal District Court and the same Judge Owens. To perfect his brief, he turned for assistance to Palmer Singleton and to Robert McGlasson, then in the 83 Poplar Street office.

Judge Owens rose to the occasion. He restated as unequivocal that "every person imprisoned as a result of a state court conviction [has] the right to file a petition in a United States district court alleging that the conviction is in violation of the Constitution or laws . . . of the United States."[11] Then, briefly disposing of six of Amadeo's other contentions of irregularity, Owens wrote with clarity on the matter of the composition of the jury. He said Amadeo could not be faulted for not raising the issue in his trial as his lawyers had no knowledge of the as-yet-undiscovered memorandum: "To overlook this act of intentional underrepresentation—and hand selection of those blacks who did serve—. . . would indeed be a miscarriage of justice." On this point (and the use by the prosecutor of criminal charges filed against Amadeo in Alabama), he ordered a new trial.

Uncowed, Putnam County justice fought back. The state appealed and the 11th Circuit overruled Owens. The next step for Tony Amadeo was to turn to the United States Supreme Court. Strong egos are not in short supply in the legal profession, but not every down-the-street lawyer is undaunted at the prospect of walking into the majestic courtroom of the Supreme Court and facing nine all-powerful justices. And so it was not Warner, but Bright, his self-confident, articulate, downtown Atlanta neighbor, who would argue the case, if the Court would agree to hear it.

Palmer Singleton wrote what has been called a "masterful" petition for certiorari, a request to be heard. He pointed out that usually even flagrant defiance of prohibitions against gender and racial bias in jury selection can be known only by "inference." No matter how persuasive statistics might be in suggesting discrimination, how could you be certain that discrimination took place? But here in the memorandum Coates had found was an actual device for denying African Americans seats on juries. There was a smoking gun.

The petition was filed on August 10, 1987; to Amadeo's new lawyers' great surprise, it did not languish, but was granted as soon as the court reconvened in the fall. Now the pressure was on. The center lawyers were in the midst of another trial and asked for a postponement, which was denied. So, for three weeks, working night and day, the brief arguing that Amadeo deserved a new trial was crafted. Robert McGlasson and Ruth Friedman worked with Singleton and Bright to perfect the argument, and reaching out to friends beyond Atlanta, subjected it to the critical eye of a "savvy" Washington, D.C., lawyer, David Reiser. Reiser was ruthless with what he thought would not persuade, insistent on that which would.

Now, perhaps, the unwritten words would work, but what about their sound? In lawyer language, Bright "mooted" the argument with two sets of trial lawyers in Washington and one in New York. There, Anthony Amsterdam, famous for his skill before the Supreme Court, and currently teaching law at the New York University School of Law, put on the nine hats of the Supreme Court justices and subjected Bright to withering questioning. Other members of the team took careful notes and the proposed oral argument was fine-tuned again.

The feverish preparation behind them, the group flew to Washington. But if the behind-the-scenes rehearsals had been exhaustive, there was still the great stage on which the drama was to be played. Onto it walked William Warner, Palmer Singleton, Robert McGlasson, and Stephen Bright to take their seats at the counsel's table in the Supreme Court of the United States. It takes more than a courtroom to intimidate Palmer Singleton, for whom trials are his life, but even he admits to awe that morning as he heard the center's first Supreme Court case called for hearing.

The Supreme Court Building can seem the true home of republican virtue—as it did on a day in May 1954 when a triumphant Thurgood Marshall, with his team of fellow lawyers, walked out into the light and down its great flight of stairs to celebrate the new law of the land designed to end segregation. But back up those stairs in the darker interior of that same building, nothing can better reflect the law's propensity for intimidation than the Renaissance solemnity of its courtroom.

Stern but obsequious ushers seat lawyers admitted to the bar of the Supreme Court up front; people concerned with the cases to be decided and argued file in behind, while tourists shuttle silently in and out in the rear. Sitting in the pit, you gaze upward at the wall of bench before you and rise in instant obedience as the antique prologue, "Oyez, oyez," is intoned. From behind a parted curtain appear the nine black-robed justices. In hierarchical order, they scurry sedately side to opposite side to their appointed chairs. Lastly, the chief justice presents himself at the center and all are seated.

That morning, Justice Thurgood Marshall, on the Court since 1967, sat, appropriately, next to William Brennan, who as the senior associate justice was on the chief justice's right. The only justice who had, in his practice, gotten to the grit of America's criminal justice system, Marshall peered intently at Bright as he argued that Joseph Briley, the Putnam County prosecutor, had broken the law that held that a person could not be excluded from a jury on account of race.

Marshall was attentive, too, to the argument of Susan V. Boleyn, assistant attorney general for the state of Georgia, who sought to defend the Georgia criminal justice system from federal interference. Marshall's jowled face was inscrutable, Warner noted, as he "studied . . . every little look and inflection" of the faces of the two lawyers.[12] He said not a word during the justices' interrogation of the lawyers.

As the story unfolded, an incredulous Justice Byron White asked, "There's never been any action against the prosecutor [District Attorney Briley]?" No, Boleyn replied, he was still on the job. The entire bench broke into laughter when she admitted his action as a little discriminatory and Justice John Paul Stevens asked, "Just a little bit pregnant?"[13] The assistant attorney general had not had a good day.

Stephen Bright fared better. Among those silently cheering as he argued his first Supreme Court Case were his mother, father, grandmother, sister, and nephew, who had come from Kentucky. One member of the team sitting near the back of the room recalls looking forward and spotting "a patch of redheads" listening intently.[14] What they heard was the law at its best. Justice Blackmun is reported to have said to his clerks later that Bright's was the finest oral argument he heard that term.

Marshall wrote the blunt decision overturning the 11th Circuit's findings refusing a new trial for Amadeo. Astonishingly, in light of future opinions, all eight of his colleagues agreed. There was a sliver of light under the door; Tony B. Amadeo was to have a new day in court.

The Putnam County judicial and prosecutorial community had been caught with a great deal of egg on its face. Instead of wiping it off with an admission of blame, they backed farther into the corner of the courthouse. Joseph Briley, whom nine Supreme Court justices had found reprehensible, remained on the case when Tony Amadeo was reindicted. On the other hand, the Superior Court judge, ignoring the fact that Amadeo had counsel that had demonstrated reasonable competence before the United States Supreme Court, appointed two inexperienced local lawyers to represent Amadeo in his murder trial. He did so straight in the face of the fact that Warner had been Amadeo's lawyer for years and Bright had successfully represented this client before the nation's highest court. When they protested, the judge stood by his decision.

This was outrageous on the face of it; but outrage doesn't get you very far in the law. Ruth Friedman, in the days before legal research could be done with the great help of the computer, went down to the Georgia State Library a few blocks away and began going through tome after tome of legal rulings. As she puts it, in capital work, "you have to have a hunger"; in this instance, "you are so angry and it's so right" that Amadeo should be allowed to keep his lawyers, that you don't give up.[15] You find the key. Finally, in a volume of California cases, she came upon a finding that, basically, said you can't treat a defendant that way. With this single precedent in hand, she prepared a brief and the Georgia Supreme Court reinstated Bright and Warner as Amadeo's attorneys.

With the trial date set, it was to be Bright against Briley. Briley was prickly. The Marshall opinion rankled. The attention in the Atlanta press to his memorandum and its discovery was embarrassing, but in his part of Georgia the episode might fade unless this new trial was to turn the spotlight back on. Set to begin, Bright had his team of lawyers and a battery of witnesses all ready to go. When he got to the courthouse, he was told that District Attorney Briley wanted to see him.

Briley had a proposition: He would agree to a guilty plea from Amadeo, with a prison term for murder. In return, he would not go to trial asking for the death penalty. Tony would escape the electric chair. Bright accepted. When Judge Hugh P. Thompson announced the agreement in the courtroom, "family members of Amadeo's 62-year-old victim, James Turk, Sr. cried."[16]

There was, however, one more piece of business: Bright,

Warner, and the team of lawyers would have to forego any fee that the county might be assessed. This the lawyers had agreed to as well. But on this one, Briley had miscalculated. When this detail of the plea bargain was made public, there was a huge outcry. Briley had not escaped further notoriety. Members of the legal establishment rose to condemn the use of fee money in such a plea. The Georgia Bar Association conducted an ethics hearing on the matter. About all Briley could say in response was: "I thought of it more as a joke."[17] Bright, of course, as party to the agreement was as guilty of a breach of propriety as Briley. He confessed: "I knew . . . that the offer was unconscionable and possibly illegal, but we had a young man's life at stake, so what were we going to do?"[18] In the face of the ethics finding that he could seek a fee, he refused. He had made the deal and would stick by it.

IN PHILLIPS STATE prison in Buford, Tony Amadeo has a vivid recollection of all of the legal team that achieved his life sentence, but the most telling memory for him now is the slim brochure made up of Stephen Bright's argument before the Supreme Court, the legal telling of that bit of the Amadeo story that prompted Thurgood Marshall to grant the order.

Stories, in fact, are now Amadeo's life work. He has his own to tell and others to devour. Sitting in a chair, his feet propped up on the windowsill—the other prisoners understand that this is Tony's space—he reads. Long ago it was the Penguin classics and Aristotle; out of who can know where, Procopius. Recently, there has been a lot of Dickens and other authors, too. *Les Misérables* is his favorite novel.

Prisoners who don't read, who play cards and, endlessly, watch television, ask him what he's reading that stuff for and he tells them the book's story. When I saw him, Tony was reading *Moll Flanders*. With Moll, there is plenty that is salacious to tell, but what Tony sees is a story closer to his own. Her mother was hanged—for petty thievery—as soon as Moll was born; Moll herself barely escaped the same end. Almost as miraculous as Moll's reprieve is his own. If she traded the English noose for a world outside, Amadeo exchanged Georgia's demanded retribution for his crime for a life within prison.

Twenty years later, Tony Amadeo reads and remembers. Every day, he fires a pistol and James Turk slides off the right side of the truck to the ground, screams for help, and dies.

10

Morgan County Courthouse

TONY AMADEO IS still alive; in 1990, William Brooks was not sure how long he would be. In January, he went on trial for his life for the second time, this time in a Georgia County courtroom in which, not a long time later, Sam Waterston would be the lawyer arguing for racial justice in the television world of *I'll Fly Away*. A local fireman was recruited to play a juror in that trial, but William Brooks could count on no one speaking a scripted line that would save a black man's life. He faced the nonfiction of jurors with the very real power of finding him guilty of murder—and ordering that he be killed. His chance, in their hands, was likely to be his last.

The Morgan County Courthouse stands at the far corner of the central square in Madison, the county seat. Handsome white antebellum houses mingle with late Victorian cottages down either side of Main Street. The Morgan Madison Cultural Center, with its tongue and groove–walled concert hall, is a proud symbol of the community that the county and town combine to be. School buses from across the county and its only other town, Rutledge, roll into Madison and its high school. People choose

Madison, surrounded by beautiful sloping fields, as a civilized place to live. An interstate brings the town within an hour's drive from Atlanta, but it is no suburb.

William Brooks had never been in Madison before his trial there. He had been sentenced to death back home in Columbus in 1977 for the murder of Carol Jeannine Galloway. Since taking Brooks's case, Stephen Bright and George Kendall had kept their client alive by dogged perseverance and a remarkable set of legal moves. Now, in 1990, he stood once again indicted for that crime. This time the prosecutor, Douglas Pullen, had to drive up from Columbus, while Bright, Kendall, and company came over from Atlanta to begin State of Georgia v. William Anthony Brooks.

The jurors in the first trial had all been white citizens, a factor in the successful appeal that occasioned this new trial. To avoid giving grounds for yet another appeal, it was incumbent on Pullen not to strike too many black jurors. This was an advantage to Bright, with his African American defendant, but he could not be certain how dependable that assist would be. As any criminal lawyer will tell you, however hard you try to craft a favorable jury with biographical information, intuition, and adroit use of strikes—refusing to seat a particular person—the result remains a matter of luck.

But having never given less than total attention to the long process of keeping William Brooks alive, no one at 83 Poplar Street was willing to trust merely to luck. If statistically the two counties of the Brooks trials, Muscogee and Morgan, were similar in proportions of black citizens to white, a key factor in the choice of Morgan for the moved trial, sociologically they were worlds apart.

Morgan is a quiet county; rural, but not backward. It long has been gentler than Muscogee. True, Morgan has its own record of lynching: Brown Washington was killed in the presence of a mob in 1890 and Wallace Baynes in 1919. Both men were black. Things are markedly different since the civil rights movement. If Madison is a town not without the usual community petty meannesses, it has a reputation for tolerance. In contrast, the city of Columbus, Muscogee's county seat, has far less of a reputation for racial justice. There civility is a fragile barrier against the culture of violence nurtured by nearby Fort Benning's special forces militarism and the nation's School for America's training in counterrevolutionary torture, as well as the legacy of racism bequeathed by its own city history. The integration of Morgan County's one quite good high school in Madison was achieved peaceably, and student relationships continue to be reasonably comfortable.

But however encouraging the site of the new trial, as little about the jury was going to be left to chance as possible. Among all the discarded motions, Bright had salvaged one. The judge ordered each juror to be examined individually and out of the hearing of the others. This accomplished, he put the investigators to work to ensure that they knew as much about each as possible, to be alert to anyone likely to be immutably committed to the death penalty.

Rising to the challenge, Gay Nease and Mary Eastland drove the fifty miles to Madison, probably at record speed—firmness on the accelerator matches the thrust of determination of this crowd. Turning off the interstate, past the short strip of the usual motels and fast-food places and onto tree-lined Main Street, they reached the courthouse and got a list of the 125 citizens who had been called for jury duty. There was a breakdown of that list, horizontally, into six age categories: 18–24, 25–34, 35–44, 45–54, 55–64, 65 and over; and then vertically: white males, white females, black males, black females, with the percentage of each category tabulated. The list was further broken down into panels—to be called in order until a jury was selected.

Beginning with the names of those on the panels that would be called first, from which the jury would probably come, they turned to the slim county telephone book for addresses, and with other more difficult digging into county records began to sketch, with their notes, portraits of each of the forty-six people on the first panels that would be called. Mary and her friend, Lewis

Sinclair, long active in civil rights activities, visited with a friend of his who also had been active in the movement in Morgan County to get his reading of those whom he knew.

As they drew others in the county into conversation, the two investigators, good at chatting, added sharp strokes to their profiles, relying on a rich but risky source: gossip. In this, they had the help of southerners' propensity for knowledge of kinships from which to extrapolate corollary information such as who goes to which Baptist church—and how often. Some of the wandering talk gave clues; some advice was candid. Of one possible juror, a fellow African American advised, "No, she thinks white."

Identifying facts fell into Mary and Gay's laps along the way, such as membership in the National Association for the Advancement of Colored People, a badge of honor in the black community earned not without risk during the civil rights struggle. This signified. So, on the other side of the street, did membership in the National Rifle Association.

Armed with addresses, the two women went to the county clerk's office to obtain the appraised value of each person's house and then drove—Mary at the wheel and Gay, camera poised, at the window—to take photographs of each of the prospective jurors' houses. With these illustrations, the stories grew fuller. Perhaps a woman—whose race and church and diploma from the Madison high school they already knew about—living in a ranch house, with its neat yard shaded by not too young trees, would have the requisite sense of security to be reluctant to condemn a man to death? Or, equally plausible, that same woman might be guessed to have little trouble doing so.

For three weeks, Mary and Gay sought any clue that would suggest that a prospective juror was not wedded to the death penalty as doctrine, but would be willing to look to contingencies in deciding between a death sentence and life in prison. All of these findings, gathered on an orderly sheet for each possible juror, were ready when Stephen Bright and his team of lawyers arrived at the motel at the intersection of the interstate and the road into Madison to prepare for the next day's look at the jurors themselves. Guesses about whether a juror would be with them or against them would not be undocumented ones.

At this critical juncture, it is the jurors who matter most. All the years of intricate maneuvers in the Brooks case were reduced now to Steve Bright's assignment: convincing at least one of twelve people so persuasively that William Brooks should live that he or she will hold out against any pressure from those who might favor death. The vaunted rule of law and the intricate (to the point at times of absurdity) criminal justice system constructed under that rule is, at this point in a murder trial, reduced to simplicity. The job of deciding whether a convicted felon will live or die is given, as it was to be in this case, to a manager away from her job at Wendy's and eleven of her neighbors.

With little idea of what lay before them and no idea that they had been scrutinized by Bright's associates, the prospective jurors assembled in the courthouse and were given a six-page questionnaire. Feeling as if they were back in school, they turned in their questionnaires and were told to come back tomorrow to learn whether, so to speak, they had passed.

SIX YEARS AFTER the Brooks retrial in Madison, I did some investigating myself. I sought out the jurors who were selected to find out, after the fact, just what their experience of the trial had been. On a fall day in 1995, I drove an hour south of Athens through the beautiful unbillboarded country outside Madison. The sky was a vivid blue, the air crisp as I turned up a long driveway to Gloria Crew's brick ranch house. Her husband joined us as we settled into a leisurely conversation in the living room.[1]

Mrs. Crew, an ample, friendly woman, her dark hair shot with gray, is a shift manager at Wendy's. In an old Georgia town not blessed with a nearby interstate, everyone would have seen everyone else at a luncheonette downtown. And Gloria Crew would have presided. Now, outside Madison, it's Wendy's where she knows everybody and everybody knows her. As she puts it, "I hate confrontations. In the South we've learned to agree to disagree." Old patterns linger in her speech; two young women, an alternate and juror, are the "black girls," but there is gentle observation rather than racism as she reflected on blacks being hard on blacks at Wendy's; whites can't even say bad behavior is a result of "human nature"; that is seen as an "attack."

She remembered Stephen Bright coming into Wendy's for breakfast early in the morning that she reported for jury duty. She liked him right away and, looking back, thought him a better lawyer than District Attorney Douglas Pullen. She only "wished he'd been on the other side." Articulate to the point of mocking academic stereotyping of fast-food workers, with a remarkable memory for details, Crew is unequivocal in her belief in the death penalty. If public opinion is to play a role, someday, in ending the death penalty, Gloria Crew will be hard to convince. She is genuinely a person of goodwill; it would be difficult to find a better example of the many Americans seemingly devoid of hatred who nonetheless embrace capital punishment.

A month later, I plunged deeper into Morgan County to find John Hubbard's house. The housepainter had said he was way out in the country, and so strong was my image of a small house in a sparse yard that, the first time past, I missed the handsome one-story house set well back behind a stand of tall pines bordered by a horse-country white fence. At the door, I was met by a beautiful teenage girl, toting an equally beautiful baby—hers, it turned out. She put in a call to her father and I waited (quite a while) for the expected gray-bearded grandfather.

Finally, in a spanking tall pickup, a good-looking man looking about thirty-five—he isn't much older—came ripping into the driveway. This was Johnny Hubbard. We weren't long getting to first names. Like Gloria Crew, his recall of the trial was rich in detail. The southern reputation for good storytelling was holding up. And like hers, the slant of the telling had color; he saw his world from a black perspective. And like Gloria Crew, he was anything but confrontational.

We walked past a formal dining room and into a family room with a large couch facing a matchingly large television set, and settled down at a gleaming little white plastic table for a long talk. Hubbard was wonderfully candid, and witty, but it was only much later that I realized the import of his final judgment on William Brooks's trial, on his living or dying.

My conversations with Crew and Hubbard made me eager to meet Rhonda Mealor. She too liked it out in the country. From a road cutting through woods and fields, you turn right over a cattle crossing to reach the Mealors' house. In the front yard are her husband's outboard-powered large pontooned fishing boat, a big pickup, a car alongside her child's tricycle. Inside, we sit down on a couch in her comfortable living room. Rhonda, in her late twenties, is a pretty, dark-haired white woman in a maroon sweatsuit. Friendly from the start, she tells me how perplexing it was to be summoned as a juror. Although she suspects the judge wasn't allowed to reveal much about the case or direct their thinking by being detailed about their responsibilities, she faults him: "not to be critical . . . or anything," but the judge told them little about what they were getting into, which, she feels "had a lot to do with the outcome of the case."[2]

This juror knew enough, she thought, to begin by thinking Brooks probably was guilty: "I guess everybody felt that way being it was a retrial." She had expected not to be seated—her mother-in-law was the Superior Court clerk sitting there in the courtroom—and, more generally, "being a white female and him being a black male and the victim being a white female." But she thought, and so must Stephen Bright have thought, that she would be "a fair juror."

Jury duty is the one time for many citizens that civic responsibility is more than a nebulous concept, and most respond to its call with true seriousness. Curiosity plays its part in this response, but even stronger is the lure of being required to play a part in a real human drama. Rhonda Mealor was not going to respond to her summons for jury duty by doing everything possible not to be chosen. "I didn't want to deliberately go in there and lie and say this man is guilty and I'll fry him." If this was her predilection, she put it aside. She meant it when she said she thought she could be fair when she filled out her questionnaire.

There is no avoiding the matter of race in these disputes. When I drove up to the crisp pale yellow ranch house where Rodney Gilbert lived, there were barbells with impressive weights in the open garage. Gilbert drove in right behind me in a shiny blue sports car; he stepped out, a Hollywood-handsome, lean man in his twenties—and in superb shape. I immediately noticed, as I was meant to, the gun in the holster on his hip. Small talk got me nowhere; there was anger in his face. I was not surprised to learn later that despite not objecting to the death penalty, he was not going to see yet another black man killed in Georgia, killed by Georgia, if he could help it.

In my interviews with these four jurors, and later with others, I discovered how surreal these jurors felt the experience to have been. In effect, they were told to erase everything extraneous to the evidence from their minds and then use those minds to make a judgment. Obviously this meant any gossip or stray information they might have about the crime in question. But it also meant erasing all of one's experiences, one's life, in order to comply with a legal abstraction of open-mindedness. Long afterward, the jurors, proud of having performed a civic duty, resented this sense of being regarded as players in a legal game.

In the Brooks case, the murder the jurors were to learn of would not be a routine television image to be turned off when it got too gory or too boring. They would have to hear about it in relentless detail, to look at graphic photographs of the corpse, to feel the presence of members of the family of the person who had become that corpse, to look at the man accused of killing her. Save somehow blotting everything from their consciousness, these twelve people had no escape from confronting a death. And the greater the pressure, so Stephen Bright hoped, the harder it might be to decide that a man should be killed.

The law offices at 83 Poplar Street temporarily moved into

thc Days Inn at the juncture of I-20 and the extension of
Madison's Main Street. The investigators, Nease and Eastland,
were there, as were the four lawyers who would represent
William Brooks in his trial. Stephen Bright and George Kendall
had been on the Brooks case now for ten years; their colleagues,
Gary Parker and Ruth Friedman, had not even been to law
school when Carol Jeannine Galloway was murdered.

The summer of the Galloway murder, Parker, whose father
was at Fort Benning, had just graduated from Columbus College
and was getting ready to head off to the Howard University Law
School. As he put it, the Galloway murder was the "classic horror story," the report in the paper that a young blond white
woman was missing and a black man was the suspect. "Boy
Scouts, soldiers from Fort Benning—everybody was out comb-
ing the woods around town looking for her body. You'd have
thought Sherman was coming through town."[3]

Things had changed. Parker had come back to Columbus
after law school, established a successful practice and been
elected state senator from the district that included Columbus.
Now his knowledge of District Attorney Pullen's tactics in a
courtroom was put to the task of saving William Brooks.

On the morning of January 7, 1991, the team had breakfast at
Wendy's; Steve Bright, after a cheery exchange with the manager in charge, led his troops to the Morgan County Courthouse.
District Attorney Pullen and his legal team from Columbus had
been joined by the local district attorney, Joseph Briley. His
availability may have been the reason Pullen had agreed to having the trial in Morgan County: Briley had gained more death
sentences from juries than almost any prosecutor in the state
and he knew the people in his counties well. He could advise on
who to avoid on the jury. And he did, after all, have a score to
even with Bright, who had bested him in the Amadeo case. He
sat with Pullen at the counsel table throughout the trial.

Just before William Brooks, brought from prison in Jackson,
was led into the courtroom, his chains were removed. Seated
near Judge Lawson, he looked out at the 125 citizens of Morgan

County called for jury duty. The prospective jurors looked up at the judge, who, with perfect legal correctness, told them frustratingly little about what they were there to do, but that, if chosen, their daily lives would be interrupted for, probably, a week.

There was a sense of excitement and dread among them. Curiosity and civic duty coexisted with a close to overwhelming urge to be dismissed and away from it all. They had been told it was to be a murder trial, and told almost nothing else at the voir dire—as jury selection, in French, is known. They were in for about as thorough a going over as any group of jurors has ever endured. One by one, members of the first panel totaling forty-six would be called in the hope that the jury could be achieved without moving further down the list of names.

That day and the next, as the jurors vividly recall, they were brought into the courtroom singly for a thorough "interrogation."[4] Each one, when his or her name was called, entered, was sworn to tell the truth—with its coda, "so help me God," carrying a certain weight in this deeply Baptist world—seated, and, with the man they would judge sitting facing them, asked if they had any conscientious objection to the death penalty.

Under a Supreme Court ruling, each prospective juror would have to establish to the prosecutor's satisfaction that he or she did not object to the death penalty—would have to be "death qualified," as the law grotesquely puts it—in order to be chosen. The prosecutor, asking for death, wanted to be certain that each juror could impose such a penalty. As each acquiesced, Bright and his team wondered if this was a person who could be "rehabilitated"; could they detect a sign of willingness to entertain the alternative of life, despite a commitment to the general concept of capital punishment? District Attorneys Pullen and Briley, too, had to decide how to read a "I wouldn't like to, but . . ."; a nod of assent (made verbal at the court reporter's insistence); an "if I had to . . ."[5]

Anyone who did flatly object to the death penalty, or had an excuse Judge Lawson accepted, had been allowed to go home as the judge, the district attorney, and the defense lawyer questioned each person, often at considerable length. The process would take seven days.*

Gloria Crew recalls Bright, having spotted an answer about her family on the questionnaire, asking her about her daughter's college. "Doesn't Bob Jones University practice segregation?" he asked. She came right back at him: "They don't allow interracial dating, but there are students there from all over the world. They live in the same dorms." Was she a good risk for his African American client? Which way would her family's choice of Bob Jones, a fundamentalist Christian school, make her lean? Asked later why she believed Bright did not strike her, she replied, "I think he thought I came across as honest."[6]

In their motel in the evenings of each day of jury selection, the four lawyers, coached by Mary Eastland and Gay Nease, began matching guesses. Far into the night, Magic Markers in hand, the group matched the investigators' sheets and the handwritten responses to the questionnaires with their impressions of what each juror had said during his or her turn in the courtroom. Munching on potato chips and devouring barbecue sandwiches, Gary Parker broke into the seriousness by kidding the "health folk" about their "damned apples and yoghurt."[7]

Canary yellow smeared across a fact on the questionnaire or on the investigators' sheet served as a warning or a possibility. "I don't like him at all," was one comment on an older white man; "Seems like a nice guy," another wrote about the same person. Where would that leave Bright when the strange game of strikes began? The one person he would most be on guard against would be a "leader"—one whose force of personality would carry the others with him or her to a unanimous choice of execution in the penalty phase.[8] Just such a potential leader would be high on Bright's strike list.

When jurors in the Timothy McVeigh Oklahoma bombing case were interviewed, several of them talked admiringly of the foreman's ability to order the proceedings and to push efficient-

*The transcript of this process fills six volumes.

ly for the verdict in both the guilt and the sentencing phases of the trial.

In another, far more controversial case—the first in New York State since the restoration of the death penalty in which the prosecutor asked for the death sentence—the jury chose execution for a decorated former correctional officer who murdered three people in a nightclub. With his admirable record, the fact that this was his first crime, and a record of mental disorder at the time of the shooting, there would seem to have been a powerful set of mitigating circumstances in Darrel Harris's behalf. Some of the jurors apparently thought so, too. At one point a court official had to enter the jury room when he heard a scuffle; two jurors were holding back a third threatening to hit a fourth. Even more telling was the uncontrollable weeping and near breakdown of a woman juror as the death sentence was pronounced. Indications are that some forceful person capable of browbeating doubters was in that jury room.

With the examination of individual jurors finally over, the silent drama of strikes began. Under the law, Bright had twenty strikes; Pullen ten. Both men had to use their strikes with the utmost discretion, based on the shrewdest hunches. The process is one of getting rid of, not choosing. The jurors were again summoned to the courtroom, this time collectively, and, one by one, asked to stand. As each stood, the clerk of the court handed a piece of paper with the names in order to Pullen, who either let the name stand, or, crossing it out, initialed it as strike 1. The clerk then took the paper from him and walked over to Bright's table, where Bright followed suit.

The juror, not knowing whether he or she would be chosen, sat and another stood. This performance went on, in silence, until the clerk counted enough uncrossed-out names and told the judge he had a jury, with three alternates.* The list com-

---

*Alternates were similarly selected. In Georgia, alternates know that they will have a vote only if someone on the jury has to leave it. In some states, they do not know of their likely redundancy until the actual deliberation begins.

piled, the judge read the fifteen names of the jurors selected, thanked and excused the others, and had the chosen jurors escorted to their seats on the platform that is the jury box in the Morgan County courtroom.

Nine black people and three white, seven men and five women, became an odd, inescapable community. There are few examples of social intercourse more intriguing than to watch a newly formed jury escorted into a local restaurant and seated together at a long table, under the eyes of a deputy sheriff. One woman tries earnestly, but with little luck, to make polite small talk; a man furtively turns, wondering whether to reach for or ask for the salt—or forgo it altogether; eyes dart, then duck. But come together the twelve must.

With the Brooks jury, there was an awkwardness—or perhaps graciousness—of another sort. Rather than being strangers each to the other, everyone here in little Morgan County knew almost everyone else. Or, more precisely, knew at least one other person on the jury. The connections made a rich mosaic. One young male juror had as his roommate, in the sequestering motel, the older deacon in a church that he sometimes attends; with a glint in his eye, the younger man told me he had "dated" one of the women. Rhonda Mealor, in addition to being the daughter-in-law of the clerk of the court, had worked in a fast-food store with Gloria Crew and been in high school with Rodney Gilbert, who worked in the same computer parts plant with alternate Larry Johnson, whose sons had had another juror, Juanita Jones, as their teacher.

Far from being that neutral body of objectivity the law imagines, these twelve people were, of course, intensely real human beings. That was evident as one after another recalled "something between a scream and a groan" heard from the hall as one of their number was on the telephone.[9] His former wife was calling to report, from the hospital, that their child had just been diagnosed with leukemia and was close to death. He pleaded to be excused totally, rather than temporarily as Bright urged on the judge—the trial was already in the sentencing phase. Judge

Lawson sent him to his family and replaced him with alternate Larry Johnson.

The jurors' humanity was tested in another way. They were sequestered, two to a room, for eight days in the Travelodge motel. The motel is no more and a little less than hundreds of thousands of its cousins at such intersections with interstates nationwide. The jurors had one stretch of the hall to themselves. There were card tables for checkers and card games and a television set on which they saw video films, the selection narrowed by the bailiffs to avoid any involving murder. The only news they were permitted was the McNeil/Lehrer NewsHour, which eschewed death other than en masse in international slaughter. The local news channels in Atlanta that thrive on local crime coverage were forbidden.

The bailiffs overseeing the jurors were from Muscogee County. They were not privy to local gossip, which limited conversation more or less to discussions about what films they wanted to see. The jurors report that the bailiffs were reasonably thoughtful and polite. They kept their views of Brooks to themselves—until after the trial.

The jurors had been told strictly that there was to be no discussion of the case. Any inclination to do so would have been curbed by the bailiffs in the hall; but what happened when the roommates retired? One juror who did not have a roommate wondered if there was talk in the bedrooms; another reported that he and his roommate never talked about the case. (Their silence was abetted by the fact that the elder of the two snored and the younger went to bed early to get a head start on some undisturbed sleep.)

The jurors would recall the dinners—over and over again—at the Western Sizzlin' Steak House across the street where other patrons complained when the salad bar was cordoned off while the sequestered jurors piled chickpeas and pickled beets on the iceberg lettuce. And jurors recalled the evenings of desultory card games and the video someone else selected. The Wendy's manager told how she was the only one who read; she had brought her Bible and a *Readers' Digest* volume of abridged books—which a bailiff took away, because one story involved a murder.

The lax evenings were crowded out by the intense days in court. When the guilt phase of the trial began on Wednesday, January 16, District Attorney Douglas Pullen opened with an effective description of the murder of Jeannine Galloway, a story as new and gripping to this new jury as it was well known, over years now, in his home county. On the witness stand, Mrs. Galloway recalled the anguish of a mother at the strange, curiously placid abduction of her daughter. Pullen brought the jurors to imagine the terror and humiliation of the daughter as she is made to strip and have her abductor's penis forced into her vagina, of the slow—perhaps, he suggests, conscious— dying as the bleeding from the wound continued after the killer fled. Photographs of Jeannine's dead body, her glasses demurely still on her nose, lying in the leaves in which she was found—and, in the laboratory, revealing the wound and the blood from it soaked into her naked back—make vivid her death.

William Brooks's fingerprints on Jeannine Galloway's car alone made it difficult for Stephen Bright to claim his client's innocence. It is a rule of his that you do not expend all of your credibility in the guilt phase of a trial with implausible arguments in a case in which you do not have a strong chance of winning. Had he been prepared to make an all-out effort to convince the jury that Brooks was not guilty, he would, for example, have to weigh in strongly with a challenge to Mrs. Galloway over her misidentification, in the police lineup, of Morris Comer as the man she had seen leaving her house with her daughter. For Bright to press Hettie Galloway after her wrenching description of her daughter's abduction would scarcely endear the lawyer to the jurors.

In Bright's view, it is essential for a defense lawyer in a death penalty case to be constantly mindful of the possible sentencing phase, as the guilt phase proceeds. What Bright did do was seek to raise a reasonable doubt in the jurors' minds about whether the gun was fired accidentally, whether Jeannine Galloway's death was caused without sufficient malice to constitute murder punishable by death.

The three days of evidence in, the final pleas heard, the court reconvened on January 19, and Judge Lawson read the charge to the jurors from the standard form required by Georgia law. They were to find William Brooks either guilty or not guilty of the charge of "malice murder." (In Georgia, the definition of the worst form of murder does not require premeditation; it does require intent, no matter how short the time the malicious intent may have existed.) There were no lesser charges, such as manslaughter, that they could convict Brooks of. They could conclude only that he was guilty or not guilty.

They were to choose the former only if the state had proven guilt, in the familiar phrase (which may not previously have been familiar to all the jurors) "beyond a reasonable doubt." Judge Lawson explained the phrase by not explaining it: "A reasonable doubt is a doubt for which a reason can be given."[10]

Alone in the jury room, the jurors, full of the details of the crime they had just heard, were still mystified as to where the story that each held of the crime fitted into the total narrative of the defendant's life. Why, they wondered, hadn't the original trial settled things? Like students, they had been admonished to pass the examination given them in the morning's stern and clear (but not simple) charge by Judge Lawson. But without the teacher in the room, they were free to try to make sense out of their differing personal responses to the contrasting stories of the crime.

Having been silent in the courtroom for days, unable to talk about what was most on their minds in their eight evenings together, now they could pour it all out on each other. The foreman, whom the group had already chosen, was Alonzo Clark, a dignified older African American Baptist deacon, and one of the two senior males of the group. The other was J. B. McLain. The eldest juror, at sixty-nine, was Mary Lizzie Park.

McLain, the white man written off by one of the Bright guessing team as an untrustworthy old boy, had been a juror on a major trial before, knew something of the law, and kept the deliberations in order—or tried to. Hubbard called him "the peacemaker," and Mealor recalls that "when things would get a little rowdy, he would say, 'Everybody sit down, calm down a little bit.' "[11] He was not, however, the "leader" so feared by Bright, one who could browbeat his fellows and press them, unwillingly, into the unanimity required for the imposition of the death penalty in Georgia. One holdout meant a life sentence. But this was a fact they did not know. (Defense attorneys are not permitted to mention the point.) All along, these jurors thought they needed a unanimous decision not only for a death sentence but for a sentence of life in prison as well.

After two hours, Foreman Clark, at the door of the jury room, handed the bailiff a question for the judge: "Do the jury make the sentence?"[12] After Judge Lawson listened to the lawyers bicker over how he should reply, he sent the jurors out for lunch. When they resumed, he read them the same instruction that he had read in the first place: They decided guilt now; if not guilty, the trial was over; if guilty, they would then meet to decide the sentence.

In the gingerbread house of legal procedure, the decisions were separable; on the evidence, the jurors should decide if Brooks was guilty or not guilty, period. In a real room in a real place these people, already pretty sure William Brooks had killed Jeannine Galloway, could not disconnect such a finding from its result. What then would happen to Brooks? If the rule book was still a mystery, these people knew what the score was there on the field.

The turf was flying. Sounds of arguments escaped through the closed door. Gary Parker called it "screaming"—possibly a good sign.[13] Defense attorneys pray for juries that don't agree. That afternoon, after what cannot have been a cozy lunch, there were more arguments; once, the bailiff knocked on the door asking them to be more quiet. Some opinions were given loudly enough to be heard in the courtroom where one more time the Galloway family and the Brooks family waited—apart.

In the years since Jeannine's death, Randolph Loney, a personable minister whose farm is just north of Columbus (and who counsels on death row every Friday and spends final hours and minutes with those who are electrocuted), had called on Mrs. Galloway seeking her forgiveness for William, to the extent of not again seeking his death, but to no effect. Brooks, too, wanted to make an overture; "I told Randy and Steve that I wanted to do that,"[14] but they told him that Mrs. Galloway was so upset that it would be counterproductive if he were to write to her.

The closest any link came to occurring between the two Columbus families happened in the hall outside the courtroom. William's five-year-old niece, Ashly, slipped and hit her head on the edge of a bench. As the mother, his sister Gwen, reached down to comfort the crying child, she looked up to see just a glimmer of compassion on Mrs. Galloway's face.

AT 3:20 THAT Saturday afternoon the jury sent word that they had reached a verdict. Prolonging the suspense, the lawyers approached the judge's bench. Out of the hearing of all but the judge and prosecutor—and the clerk—Bright said, "Your honor, since we're going to a penalty phase," he would ask that the jury be polled. Judge Lawson asked with mock curiosity, "Why do you think we're going to a penalty phase? . . . That's not very optimistic." Bright, recovering, "No, I expect the worst and wait to see what happens."[15]

With William Brooks and his lawyers sitting at their table, District Attorney Pullen and his staff at theirs; with Jeannine's mother and father, William's mother, sister, and niece in the visitors' pews, the jurors reentered the court. Alonzo Clark passed their written verdict to the clerk, who read out, "Guilty." In the polling, Foreman Clark gave Bright only the weakest clue as to what had been said in the jury room. The preacher, concurring in the verdict, added: "It was a tough decision, but it was my own."[16] Beyond this, Bright had no way of knowing what the jurors had said to each other as he turned to the sentencing phase of William Brooks's trial.

11

"Just Plain Mean"

O N THE MORNING of Monday, January 21, 1991, lawyers, jurors, and a client named William Anthony Brooks drew near a death. As they had each day of the trial, the jurors, waiting for the start, could hear, just outside their jury room, the clank of the chains as they were unfastened from Brooks's legs and dropped to the floor. This morning he would be led into the courtroom and they would take their seats for the phase of the trial that would determine his sentence. Since the judge was reluctant to hold court on a Sunday, the jurors had been sequestered over the weekend. Their only outing was to be a trip to church, a bailiff accompanying them. Since this was Baptist country, the number of their churches probably matched their own number, but they had to pick just one to attend. Somehow one was found that satisfied.

On Monday, Stephen Bright put William Brooks's mother on the stand, and, telling again the story of her brother's savage beatings as a child, his sister Gwendolyn. (One juror recalls that another was visibly upset at the graphic description.)[1] Bright then had Dorcas Bowles, an expert in the field of child abuse with impressive professional credentials, testify as to the lasting effects of such treatment. Bowles, firm and articulate, stood up with quiet resolution against Pullen's strenuous cross examination: "So, you're telling me that a conduct of a child is not his own responsibility, that he is merely a product of what the folks that raised him did." Bowles answered, "He is a product of the interaction between himself and his parents and the environment." "Do you accept phrases like a child being spoiled?" "Yes, a child can be spoiled." "How about a brat?" "A child can be a brat." "Some of them just plain mean?" "Not without reason." "Suppose they just want to be mean?" She would not follow him into having Brooks made intrinsically evil; "Children usually are responsive to the interaction . . . between them, their parents and others in their environment."[2]

Building a case that Brooks's whole life, not just the day of the murder, should be considered in the decision whether he should go on living, Bright put a minister, Randolph Loney, on the stand. Loney, who had counseled Brooks in jail, told of the prisoner's contrition and of his good behavior in his years as an inmate. But Loney, as a minister to men on death row, had long been a thorn in the prosecutor's side and Pullen treated him with withering scorn as a meddling do-gooder.

On Wednesday, January 23, 1991, the mitigating and aggravating stories told, the jurors were to hear District Attorney Pullen give the closing statement for the state and Stephen Bright for the defendant. These two men would give voice to William Brooks's fate; he, who had not testified, could only sit, watch, and wait. The lawyers had active tasks before them. For them, the question of Brooks's life or death was a matter of language. The two men were as articulate as William Brooks, with his stutter, was not. The answer to the question of whether he would live or die would, it seemed, depend on how jurors read the words they spoke.

Sitting silently in their separate chairs, the jurors would indeed listen, but theirs was anything but a passive role. Not one of these twelve Georgians was a replica of the statue of Justice playing hide-and-seek, with kerchief blindfolding her eyes, balance scale in hand, weighing aggravation against mitigation. These jurors lived in the real world of sympathy, vengeance, compassion, retribution, privilege, deprivation; they had gone to school, dropped out of school, made love, failed in love, gotten jobs and lost them: they knew what it was to be white, to be black in Georgia.

They brought all of this baggage into the Morgan County Courthouse that morning. The baggage was a burden, yes, but it was crammed with the stuff of life that these twelve people would bring to making a decision about another life. Douglas Pullen and Stephen Bright were, in the opinion of Gary Parker, who knew them both well, "as different as two lawyers can be." Pullen affected the "rough and brash manner of a street fighter," and let his emotions spill over into the courtroom in his exchanges with the judge. Bright was "a surgeon, always in control," who would "never lose his temper or raise his voice." Faced with a judge's adverse ruling, he would insist on a full clarification. He wanted to be "aware of any land mines he might step on."[3] Parker's assessment was echoed by Rhonda Mealor; Bright, she recalled, was always "on the ball. I don't imagine anybody of this jury could sit there and say that he was not the best lawyer in that courtroom."[4]

It was after eleven on the morning of January 23, 1991, when the testimony of witnesses in the sentencing phase was completed; it was time for the two lawyers' closing statements. Judge Lawson asked the jurors if they wanted to break for lunch or press on. He explained that the two might take as much as a total of four hours, after which they would have to deliberate. With the thought of possibly another night in the motel, they quickly chose to skip lunch.

Pullen went first. After thanking the jurors for serving, he reminded them of promises "that each and every one of you made me" that you were not opposed to the death penalty. You "owe it to me, to this court, to our State, to this defendant and to those people who loved Jeannine Galloway to consider fairly and fully the death penalty."[5]

The district attorney now made sure that the horror of the death of Jeannine Galloway was clearly before the jurors. In 1977, William Brooks deprived her of any further time on earth, of a marriage, of a life. And the jury had seen that he had cruelly deprived a fiancé and a mother, both of whom were present in the courtroom. Pullen was determined to fix Brooks in the jurors' minds solely at that single terrible, destructive moment in his life, the murder of Jeannine Galloway.

Pullen sought to erase Brooks's life before the murder by attacking those who had testified that William Brooks was terribly damaged. He scorned the sister who had wrestled her way out of the terrible situation at home and gotten an education and a middle-class job: "When the defendant started getting in trouble, she was busy graduating from high school and didn't even pay any attention to it."[6] Had he thought how this would play with the African American jurors?

Trying to minimize Brooks's sister Gwendolyn's description of the beating of the child by the stepfather, Pullen admitted that his "heart went out to that woman." But then he went on to differentiate her good conduct, her becoming "a productive member of society," from that of her brother. "I am not going to debunk child abuse," he insisted, but "there is only so far that child abuse will go to excuse . . . somebody's conduct."[7]

"We heard from the mother, and she loves him in her own way. We heard from his sisters and they love him. We heard about the horrible beating at the hands of [his stepfather]. If it were half as bad as they described, which of us would have blamed William Anthony Brooks for killing him? But William Anthony Brooks did not take out his criminal conduct on a person who had harmed him but on a hundred-pound innocent and defenseless woman."[8] Constantly, Pullen sought to get the jury to see William and Jeannine on facing pages. Her death must be matched by his.

After a brief recess, the jurors came back into the courtroom to hear Stephen Bright. He rose, walked over to the jury box, and fixing his eye on each of these residents of Morgan County in turn, said, "We get down now to the ultimate issue here. Do we kill William Brooks?"[9] "Kill" is the word and "we" are the killers.

Bright had not constructed a universal "we," so broad as to encompass everyone—and no one. Rhetorically, he made himself party to the process, but his point was that the twelve to whom he spoke were that "we." Responsibility for Brooks's death could not be passed along to some "other"—not to the state, to the murderer who brought it on himself, to a rule of law. Firmly, Bright reminded the twelve sitting before him that they would decide whether or not to kill William Anthony Brooks. "I've never been in the position . . . you are in. This young man's life is in my hands now, but it will soon be in your hands."[10]

Then, more conversationally, he told them, "I want to just talk to you for the next little bit." He spoke of their patience, of the delay in their lunch, but, "obviously, we're down to the most important thing in the world here for William Anthony Brooks and . . . for these members of his family sitting here on the front row. . . ."[11] He had formally named his client, who, as he speaks, will be neither some synonym for victim nor, bleakly, "the defendant," but—unabashedly, personally—William Brooks."

The choice was between "death by electrocution, the elimination of human life by 2200 volts of electricity, or imprisonment for the rest of one's natural life." But not, in another sense, a "natural life." ["W]e're not talking about . . . life to stroll the streets, life to play with our kids, life . . . to live our lives, to see the birds, to go fishing. . . ." What lies ahead, if not death, is life imprisonment. "All through this trial—I don't know if you've noticed it or not, but every day when my client, Mr. Brooks, has come to court, I know he's here because I hear the chains rattling."[12]

Bright focused directly on the members of the jury. There was no down-home folksiness; instead, respect. "Each of you is the supreme court today. You are supreme. And the decision that's in your hands, of course, is the supreme decision about whether William Anthony Brooks lives or dies." There was no pretext of lawyerly detachment: "I'm pleading for his life and you know that"; but then, as if he were going to show them a way to open a can of soup, Bright told them that he'd like "to see if I can organize things a little bit," so as to be "useful to you."[13] The issue is an ultimate one, but his tone now is calm and collegial.

"Mr. Pullen said I wouldn't talk about Miss Galloway. I'm talking right now about Miss Galloway," and Bright reaches in vain for any fresh language that can match the horror of a "terrible series of crimes that were committed. . . ." Lacking language, he reaches for rhetoric: "if we could bring Miss Galloway back, William Brooks would sit down in that electric chair. I would throw the switch myself."[14] This was rhetorical absurdity piled on impossibility, but without being explicit, he has introduced Brooks's remorse. How this rang in the jurors' ears would be hard to gauge.

Bright surely did not pause to ponder, but, glancing over to Pullen, said, "He told you" that a life sentence would be a "freebie" (about Bright's only use of slang was in this quotation). Bright insists that a life sentence is a very real punishment.[15] That slightly derisive "he" was designed to separate Pullen from Bright and from the jurors with whom he seeks to bond.

He also must make the jury aware that "no case has to be satisfied by the death penalty," and he does so with a litany of cases in which it was not obtained—a serial killer in Atlanta, the murderers of Martin Luther King, Jr., and Medgar Evers, the killing of the little girls in the Birmingham church. "Don't let anybody tell you that [there] . . . has to be a death penalty."[16] This is the only moment in the trial that Bright allows himself to speak directly to the black members of the jury; all the victims he mentions were African Americans.

Suddenly, reaching back to his Sunday School days (I suspect he had a little help here from someone who was a lot closer to Scripture), Bright took the jurors through to William Brooks. His path, in this deeply Christian part of the world, was through the Bible, with "our Savior" as his guide. His test was the parable of the seeds cast upon the rocks, to be blown away, among the thistles, to be choked out by them, and finally, to fall upon fertile ground. With William Brooks, "we're talking about somebody whose seed was not that great to begin with and it grew up among the thorns . . . and this little seed tried to struggle, two, three, four—six years old—through those thorns."[17]

As a tiny child, could William be "just plain mean," as Pullen had described him; could any child? One woman in the visitors' rows remembers the silence that engulfed the courtroom as Bright intoned, "just plain mean." He did so repeatedly: "Let's get back to that a minute. 'Just plain mean.' And I suggest to you, ladies and gentlemen, that the notion, if you buy it, denies the redemptive power of God Almighty who can change the coldest and the hardest heart. But this is not the coldest and the hardest heart. This is a troubled—a kid that had every difficulty. But this is not the coldest and hardest heart. And that notion of cold and mean denies that there's something in human nature, something in the human spirit that people can respond to. Life and faith is a journey. It's always an unfinished job. It's a long journey."[18]

Traveling back to the past, Bright reconstructs the scene of the boy "crying hysterically while his parents fought, while his older brothers and sisters fought off his dad from his mom." Pullen had said: "Well, they kissed him after it was over and . . . told him they loved him, so it made it okay." But—again with a "we"— "Do we want our child to go through even one time of seeing two human beings engaged in that kind of violence . . . ?"[19] And, building, he takes the jurors again through the still worse beating by the stepfather, and finally to the stutter—and the ridicule it provoked.

Bright has established a context for Brooks's terrible act and moves on to rehabilitation; Brooks, in part through Randolph Loney's counseling in the Jackson prison, has, Bright argues, earned a place in the city of the living. Returning to his metaphor, Bright said that if the journey stretches back into William's terrible childhood, it more essentially stretches into a future of his living: "I ask you to sentence him to the rest of his life in prison. I ask you, ladies and gentlemen, to let this rough and difficult journey go on until there it ends."[20]

Now the focus is on the jurors themselves: "I ask you to pray for the strength to give this case your individual considered judgment." Then, to that familiar line from Ecclesiastes, "For everything there is a season"—"this is a time to punish. . . . But it is not a time to kill. It is not a time to kill."[21]

IT WAS 1:40 in the afternoon; the lawyer had taken only two hours. The bailiff took the jury to lunch. An hour later, they were back and Judge Lawson read them the charge, which included the statement that "the defendant enters this phase of the trial with the benefit of the presumption that there are no aggravating circumstances which would warrant the death penalty."[22] Then, turning to what those aggravating circumstances might be, he mentions the allegation of rape and describes that crime clinically. He discusses mitigating circumstance, without reference to any specifics, and closes: "Nothing in the law forbids you from extending mercy out of compassion if you believe that life imprisonment is sufficient punishment under all circumstances." After the charge (and returning to the courtroom for a clarification) the jurors go into their room to deliberate.[23]

It would be an error to separate this second deliberation from the first. The issue of the death penalty dominated both. In the guilt phase, Rodney Gilbert had made the argument that Brooks's gun might have gone off accidentally, that he hadn't intended to kill. Rhonda Mealor, who had been sitting next to Gloria Crew, got up and took a seat right next to Gilbert: "Rodney, you've been around guns a lot, you're not naive enough to believe that gun went off accidentally."[24] But he held to the idea; we "had to go around quite a while," she recalls, until finally she said, "Okay, Rodney, you have to cock the gun, put your finger on the trigger—it's only common sense, if he really didn't intend to shoot her, why did he cock the gun?" "He was," Rhonda admits, "a tough one," but she had silenced Gilbert.[25]

If Rhonda thought there was little doubt in any mind that William Brooks had killed Jeannine Galloway, she was coming to see that there was more than a little doubt that some of the people in the room were not going to see him killed for doing so. The arguments, their sounds reaching around the door and into the courtroom, were, at bedrock, between those who thought the death penalty the correct penalty for murder, and those who were willing to go so far as to raise the possibility of an acquittal to prevent this particular person from being executed.

It was clear that in the guilt phase, in their differing ways, some, but not all, of the seven African Americans had dug in their heels. One of the white people is convinced that by the time the decision was made on Brooks's guilt, it was understood that Brooks's defenders would only vote "guilty" if there was not to be a death penalty.

Another juror feels certain that such a bargain was never stated, but recalls someone, eager that Brooks be found guilty, saying straight out, you can find him guilty and not give him the death penalty. If that was the understanding, it did not end debate as the sentence was to be decided. Rhonda Mealor insisted that if they had found him guilty, they should impose the death penalty. And the arguments intensified.

The racial makeup of the jury had shifted by one from the guilt phase to the decision on the sentence. Morris Edwards, the black man stricken by the news of his son's being diagnosed as having leukemia and dying, had been excused by Judge Lawson to be with his child. He was replaced by a white alternate, Larry Johnson (who had heard all of the evidence exactly as if he had been on the original jury). Now there were four white jurors and eight black.

Rhonda Mealor, despite—or perhaps because of—being the youngest juror, was outspoken. There was in her view no question as to where William Brooks's guilt led. She challenged her

fellow jurors to face up to this fact and give him a death sentence. She was countered by Juanita Jones, who stated her cat-
egorical dislike of the death penalty. Outraged, Rhonda thinks,
"She never should have been in that courtroom," since she must
have been asked if she could impose the death penalty, but said,
"flat out," in the jury room that she could not be responsible for
someone else's life. When she said that, Mealor turned to her:
"You shouldn't be here."[26] In her view, all of these jurors had
committed themselves to give the death penalty if the crime war-
ranted it. The murder of a raped girl (about her age and, like
Rhonda recently, planning her wedding) did so warrant.

Juanita Jones, a dignified retired longtime grammar school
teacher, known for being "real thorough" as a teacher, turned
the jury room into a classroom and lectured her pupils.
Apparently, with rising passion—"she really got upset"—Jones
turned to the mitigating circumstance of the abuse of William as
a child.

I know what Mrs. Jones contended only by talking with other
jurors.[27] When I contacted her initially, she told me very polite-
ly but firmly that the case had been too emotional an experience
for her to talk about it even so long after the event. As my conversations with her fellow jurors progressed, I came to see how
crucial she had been, but a carefully worded letter and follow-
up call received the same understandable refusal to revisit a
moment when she had given more of herself than she had ever
before been asked to give. It was in Wendy's that it all began to
make sense to me. I had met Larry Johnson there, and while we
talked, the affable man, as he described his fellow jurors unself-
consciously, never identified them racially. Of Juanita Jones, he
said, "I've always liked her." The children who were her students respected their demanding teacher, and it was clear that
Johnson did, too.

Initially, as they went around the room giving their opinions
of the death penalty, only Jones and one other person were openly opposed. It seemed to Johnson that "it could go either way."
But not when, for an hour, as he recalls it, "Miss Jones had the

floor."[28] Johnson recalls saying that he regretted that Georgia law at that time did not offer as an alternative to execution a sentence of life without parole. In an initial poll, a taking of the temperature, there seemed to be a seven–five split; the proponents of the death penalty were J. B. McLain,* Gloria Crew, Rhonda Mealor, and Larry Johnson (all white), and Angela Lowe (a black young woman about Jeannine Galloway's age).

It was then that Juanita Jones stressed the terrible effect on a child of the treatment William had been subjected to. Larry Johnson suspects that teaching small children for so many years played a part in her sensitivity to this issue—"she's seen a lot of it."† But it was not only Brooks's life before the murder that mattered to Jones; she spoke of his record in the more than thirteen years he had spent in jail. "Rehabilitation"—she used the word—was possible. "Redemption" would have been the Christian term.

As the Galloway family, the Brooks family, Pullen and Briley, and the Bright team all waited, Gary Parker recalls going down the wide flight of stairs to the bathroom and, up the stairwell, hearing one of two white old boys sitting on a bench on the first floor say, "In the old days it wouldn't have taken so long."[30]

In a second polling, the split was nine to three. Juanita Jones, the leader (however reluctant) Bright warns his law students to avoid, had won over McLain and Johnson. She persisted. Jones, the juror that someone had warned "thinks white," was thinking in vivid colors of death by electric chair and of a redeemed life.[31] Always the teacher, she even had a message sent to the

---

*Since the trial, J. B. McLain has died. There is disagreement among those recalling the deliberations. Larry Johnson thinks that he and Bryant (the farmer) were the two white people who, as opinions on the death penalty were given, were opposed to it.

†We need a "Baldus Study" of the relationship of child abuse to the death penalty, with prevention of both in mind. Executioners deal in damaged goods—damage often done long ago in the life of the person who kills and is in turn killed.

judge asking if Brooks would receive therapy for his speech impediment in jail. Finally, to stop a scolding that seemed likely never to end, Crew and Lowe reluctantly capitulated. Still, Rhonda Mealor held out. But when, ultimately, "It was one against all the rest, I realized there was no hope for the death penalty."[32] At 5:00 P.M. they sent in word by Foreman Clark that they had reached a decision.

William Brooks and Stephen Bright stood. Alonzo Clark handed the decision to the clerk, who read out (as the text appears in the official transcript): "We find the following statutory aggravating circumstances to exist beyond a reasonable doubt." Brooks's heart must have stopped as she added, "The offense of murder was committed while the defendant was engaged in the commission of a rape." But then she continued: "And notwithstanding the findings of the foregoing statutory circumstances, we find that the defendant, William Anthony Brooks, should be sentenced to life imprisonment."[33]

William Brooks gave a deep sigh. Gary Parker glanced over at Pullen as "his head drooped in utter dejection."[34] Hettie Galloway showed no emotion. "Tears welled up in the eyes of Steve Bright and he whispered a quiet thank you to the Morgan County jurors as they left."[35] Then he turned and hugged William.

Had it been this lawyer's plea that saved his client? Douglas Pullen, who was no friend to Bright or his cause, told his adversary that he had never heard so fine a piece of work. It seemed a triumph to all of the group from 83 Poplar Street. George Kendall considers it a masterpiece; it is taught in law school courses.

But the audience was not Bright's proud parents sitting in the rows of visitors' chairs, not the Galloway family, not the Brooks family, not Austin Sarat, a scholar of capital punishment who had come down from Massachusetts to see and hear Bright at work. Many who agree with Stephen Bright about the wrongness of the death penalty but are not in daily contact with it chose to hear him as speaking to a future public, one that will finally end capital punishment. But, as Bright, with his eye on his client, would agree, his audience, the one that mattered, was the jury.

When I asked several jurors what they had thought of Stephen Bright, they were impressed. Gloria Crew said that "if I were in trouble, I'd want him for my lawyer."[36] Rhonda Mealor felt that way, too, but Bright's plea made that juror "angry," dwelling as he did on Brooks's childhood; that had "nothing to do with the trial."[37] On the other hand, Larry Johnson, a proponent of the death penalty also, recalls that "it brought tears to your eyes."[38] Others, however, were curiously unimpressed with Bright's closing plea. It hadn't, they repeatedly said, made much difference. This surprised and, I confess, perversely amused me. How could so splendid a mastery of both the language and the substance of the case *not* have mattered?

I suspect it was partly a question of the passage of time and partly a comment on our culture. This is not a time when machine shop workers, beauticians, and waitresses—or for that matter elaborately educated CEOs—expect or respond to the grandeur of language. Other ways of communicating that belong to what we call popular culture speak a language that people do hear and understand. Oratory no longer does.

The memory of all the jurors to whom I spoke was of the jury room (and the motel) and the voices of their fellow jurors, particularly that of the astonishingly persistent third-grade teacher who would not let them go outside for recess. Perhaps Ruth Friedman is right; "they had already made up their minds."[39] But I am convinced that Bright's address did at least affect the climate for the final deliberation. His themes of child abuse, of rehabilitation, and, somehow, his stress on "just plain mean," were echoed that afternoon by Juanita Jones as she pressed hard against the death penalty. It is she they recall.

They recall, too, their final minutes together as a group. They had been taken back to the motel to pick up their packed things to be driven back to town and rides home. One of the Muscogee bailiffs who had kept his tongue all through the long evenings in the motel during the trial treated them to his opinion: "You know

what you've done; they'll let him go free." Suddenly, the ani-
mosity that they had contained surfaced. One "black woman
[probably Juanita Jones] called out, 'Let me off.' And she got
off."40 Another juror, sympathetic to the bailiff's point, never-
theless says he "should have kept his mouth shut."41

THE JURORS LIVE with vivid memories of William Brooks's trial,
and so do I, though I wasn't there. In one of my conversations
with John Hubbard a while back now, we had talked candidly
about many aspects of the Brooks case; but for him, it came
down to the belief that "he had no right to decide whether or not
someone dies; He [pointing skyward] does that." But Johnny, I
asked, didn't you say that you could send someone to be executed? He looked straight at me and said, "I said I could if I had
to." He paused: "But I didn't have to."42

12

Jimmy Autry State Prison

THE WILLIAM BROOKS trial was over. The jurors left the jury box, their job done. They had, it was said, denied the Galloways "closure"—the word invoked to suggest a concept of emotional completion they had sought for thirteen years. But, as one astute student of psychology has suggested, they may have been misled. If they had heard the sentence of death in the electric chair, the intoning of "May God have mercy on your soul," they would have faced the ordeal of living with the days and hours of the killing of the killer. This might have added another blinding facet to the diamond hardness of their memory.

If there never had been the possibility of a death penalty and Brooks had gone off to a life sentence in jail years earlier, a girl's mother and father, a woman's lover, might have found a quieter way in which the horror could soften—a little.

AFTER BEING ALLOWED to pose for beaming commencement day photographs with Stephen Bright and George Kendall and with his mother and sisters just after the jury's decision and the trial's end, William Brooks took off his courtroom clothes and got back into prison garb. Since leaving death row in 1991, he has been in several jails. Now he is in Jimmy Autry State Prison in south-central Georgia.

I drove south from Albany, the scene of so much civil rights history, past vast cotton fields, arching irrigation armature speaking of the technology that has replaced the ways of the Old South, and lush pecan groves that line the highway stretching flat mile after flat mile. The prison, a cluster of low-lying buildings behind razor wire, is just off Route 19.

After a good many tries, my visit had finally been sanctioned by the officials of the prison and the Department of Corrections public relations office in Atlanta. I'm shown to the warden's secretary, who introduces me to Warden Wendy Thompson and then escorts me through the prison yard, in which men, more of them black than white, are on their way back from lunch. She takes me toward a single-story building, across from another with faded lettering, LIBRARY, and we go into the offices of the prisoners' counselors.

William Brooks's counselor spots a man outside on the concrete pathway and summons him. A short, round person of about forty—cleanshaven, smooth-skinned, with a small neat mustache—comes through the door and starts past me. I call out a little tentatively, "William?" He turns and smiles. One counselor, hastily gathering up batches of forms, vacates his office. Sitting side by side, inmate EF137251 and I have a long private conversation. Early on he says, "I didn't expect you would be so old."[1]

There is no ice to break. We have talked before by telephone; once when Charlotta Norby made a lawyer's call and put me on the line, and several other times when William made the allowed nine-minute collect calls from a pay phone in a noisy common space. "Gentle" is the word that comes to mind as I recall all my conversations with him, punctuated only rarely with a stutter. Brooks does not have a probing intellect, but he is introspective and smiles readily as we talk comfortably. Like Tony Amadeo, he seems to embody Stephen Bright's familiar saying that there is more to the life of a person than the worst thing he or she has ever done.

In addition to the violence at home, his school records suggest only one teacher who (briefly) took an interest in him. William never went beyond junior high school; asked what he was doing in those high school years, he replied: "Basically doing time." From age seventeen to twenty-one he was in jail for lesser crimes, and, then, out of jail, there was the day of strange sexual hunger and the unspeakably hideous expression of how to satisfy it. And since, twenty years in jail because of that one day of terrible acts.

William Brooks, with his scanty education, has a remarkable curiosity about history that exemplifies the educational travesty of declaring, as his grade school records suggest, that he was not educable. Obviously, his troubles at home as well as his stutter had followed him into the school, but they have not made him unable to learn now. He tells me proudly of passing the high school equivalency test and receiving the certificate stating that he had. "It took me a long time to get it," he says with a triumphant laugh. "I told everybody, told Mary [Sinclair], told my mother—twice." Was she proud?" "Oh, yeah, she was—I was!" Fellow inmates were the best teachers, he says, as he plodded through the dreary workbooks in preparation for the test.

Without thinking what I was doing, I had sent William a copy of Patrick O'Brian's *Master and Commander,* and now I asked if he had read it. "Of course. Funny, some of the slang . . . the English phrases." As we talk about the arcana of rigging sails on brigantines in this seafaring book, I realize that indeed he has read it and recalls aspects of the complicated historical novel better than I did. He probably hadn't seen an ocean and I doubt if Napoleonic naval wars were high on the list of topics at junior high school in Columbus, Georgia.

I was closer to home when I sent him *An Easy Burden.* "I liked that Andrew Young book," telling of Young's days as one

of the most active of the civil rights workers in Georgia: "He
reminds me a little of Steve and his crew." William particularly
liked it when he found people he knew, like Patsy Morris, men-
tioned in the book. He said he was looking forward to meeting
her someday; I had to tell him she had died. Clearly, he thought
a good deal of her and her critical entry into his life.

Speaking of Bright, William says, "He was real professional,
had a game plan. . . . He kept me informed, except once." He
can't forget that only when he got to the Morgan County jail did
he learn that District Attorney Pullen had turned down a plea
offered prior to his second murder trial and, instead, had insisted on seeking the death penalty.

Brooks, with his life at stake, obviously kept a close eye on
all of the legal team at work: "They were great guys; George was
sort of trigger-happy . . . he would interrupt the judge and Steve
would say, you can't do that." On the other hand, one time,
Bright, ignited by something Pullen said, exploded from his
chair with "Objection" in a voice so loud it startled everyone in
the courtroom. From time to time, Ruth Friedman—"about that
tall" (he holds his hand out about five feet off the floor)—sitting
behind him at the counsel table, would reach over and whisper,
"Are you all right?" He would whisper back that he was. If he
was the silent one of the group, he, the client, was at one with
his lawyers. Long before Morgan County, Brooks had taken a
keen interest in the legal details of his lengthy appeals process,
reading and retaining details of some of the almost countless
legal documents of his case.

When I asked him about, as I put it, that day in the summer
of 1977, he responded quickly, "I never will forget it." "Can you
tell me what the hell made you do it?" He shifts into a chain of
disparate thoughts: "As I always told Steve, if I hadn't been
arrested, there's no telling what I would have done. I was about
out of it . . . I wasn't in good health." His voice drops to an
almost inaudible whisper when he says no, he hadn't known
Jeannine Galloway before the encounter in her driveway; the
only way he can put it is, "it started out to be a robbery and

became two or three other things." There the narrative stops; he won't, can't go farther. Suddenly the chairs side by side in the corner of the room, with the counselor's steel desk almost at our knees, seem far apart.

William's life as a child and a petty criminal teenager—and as a murderer—was one of chaos. I suspect that however poorly he thinks of it, prison has at least imposed an order that his life had never known. Curious if this is so, I ask, "Are you calmer now?" "Yes," he replies, but won't credit prison. "How did you achieve this steadiness?" "Basically analyzing myself. . . ." When we kid about the business of psychiatrists and their analyzing, he says, "Sometimes I'm one myself. You look at things you've done. Recognize yourself; want to make a change. . . . I know I can change."

Suddenly he startles me: "I love me." Asked what he means, he replies: "Don't get a chance to love anybody else. If you wanted to you probably could. . . . You got homosexuality in every prison. . . . I choose not to." We talk instead about friendship: "I care about most of the guys here," but, always on guard, he can claim no really close friends. His roommate is young and confused, and Brooks tries to help him out as he does other men, "when there's a death in the family, or something." Despite his childhood, William frequently speaks of family—particularly of his sister Gwen and his niece Ashly.

When I describe a one-paragraph letter, full of misspelling and grammatical errors, that I had read at 83 Poplar Street from a prisoner complaining of conditions and ending: "I had to pay to have this writ," William tells of having written letters for illiterate inmates in Autry. There is no longer any vocational training in the prison, but there is still the school and Brooks hopes he will be assigned as a teacher now that he has his GED; he will have to wait ninety days for a new assignment cycle to come around. "Better than hard labor, or something," he says with a laugh. (You get the impression that William is not much for physical exertion.) Pointing to the computer next to the counselor's desk, he says that when he gets out, he wants to study how to use one.

He is concerned about the severity of the parole system. He tells of men who, he thinks, should be out, singling out one man who has been in for twenty-four years and has a clean disciplinary record. He has told his sister he wants the name of his state senator so that he can write to him about this. He still has faith that one day he will be paroled himself: "I have a Hope scholarship* but I can't use it till I get out." And he doesn't come up for consideration again until 2004. If the present climate continues, his chances are not good. Indeed, there is movement in the legislature to end parole altogether.

Emotional response is submerged as we talk about William's time on death row. He recalls all the crocheting they used to do. (I recall being in Palmer Singleton's office one day when he opened a package to find an afghan, in loud oranges and browns, that a client had sent him.) He tells of knowing Tony Amadeo; they were in the same cell group, and when, in groups of sixteen, they were taken from their cells for three hours in the exercise yard or common room to play cards or watch television, he and Tony would talk. He remembers how smart he was.

Asked how it is when someone is taken away to be killed, he turns away—"Well, it gets quiet. I had a guy I knew on the street [in Columbus] get executed—Jerome Bowden. . . . My brother used to take up for him because he was mental . . . [here Williams stutters, recalling Bowden's deficiency]." What sort of shape was he in when they came to get him? I ask: "Jerome had faith in the people who were trying to kill him." He recalls, as so many people do, how Bowden was examined to see if he was sufficiently intelligent to be put to death: "When he took the test he did his best. . . ." Brooks's voice trails off. "He tried to get educated while he was on death row; he was a good guy." When he was taken from his cell to be readied for the electric chair, "he didn't fully realize [what was going to happen]."

He recalls one man from Carolina: "I got to know him pretty

*Governor Zell Miller's scholarship plan promises further education for anyone who graduates from high school with a satisfactory record.

good; all of us was friends. He was scared in the night; they came and got him at night for death watch . . . he was real nervous. . . ." Brooks's voice sinks again as he recalls the moment; and recalls, too, that he had been taken for deathwatch in January 1983. "Yeh, I had to prepare myself for death . . . just calm, be calm. My sister Gwen said she wanted to come to the execution. I said, you don't want to come to an execution, see somebody killed. . . . It's weird."

William Brooks got the news of his stay on the television set in the deathwatch room; simultaneously, one of the officers got a phone call and passed him the word. "We all stand up watching the TV." Were the officers happy? "I doubt it. They might have been—they're human."

13

Across Georgia

I T IS MAY 1998 and my visits to 83 Poplar Street are becoming less frequent even as my sense of being implicated increases. There have been changes. Tamara Theiss's investigating has taken a new turn; she's at law school at Northeastern University in Boston. Other voices supply the simple greeting, "Law Offices": MaShelle Epps has gone back to college; she is studying for her bachelor's degree in psychology at Georgia State University. The Tasty Town has closed to make room for yet another Georgia State expansion in the neighborhood. Even Charlotta, one of the veterans, has moved to another indigent defense office.

Tanya Greene has gotten married. Randy Loney, along with the office mafia, went out to her husband's family's in Chicago where he performed the ceremony. Her husband is a lawyer in the Atlanta public defender's office; they are expecting twins next winter. Randy, the house chaplain to these sometime pagans, also married Mary Eastland and Lewis Sinclair. Chris Johnson followed suit; he found an Athens bride and brought her to his Grant Park house—within (vigorous) walking distance of 83 Poplar Street.

Changes, of course; but things go right on. Other cases have joined Amadeo and Brooks in the cellar; finished and boxed. New ones have adrenaline riding high upstairs. When I called with a question the other day, I was told, "I'll get you the answer, but not until the week after next week. The Mike Ashley hearing has me crazy 'til then." The Supreme Court's squeezing of the rights of appeal has truncated the time the center lawyers have to work to keep their clients alive. Ashley may not have as long a span trying to hold on to that life as William Brooks did and as Carzell Moore still does.

It is now close to two and a half years since the day I drove to Henry County for my introduction to the world of the death penalty. That day, Judge Joseph B. Newton presided over the hearing to resolve issues related to the sentencing trial of Carzell Moore convicted of the 1976 murder of Teresa Allen in Cochran, Georgia. Although we were in Henry County for the hearing, the trial itself, as a result of an earlier agreement, has been moved out to the Flint Judicial District, to McDuffie County. Thomson is the county seat; it lies in east-central Georgia; just beyond it is Augusta, the Savannah River, and South Carolina.

The motions are disposed of—to no one's surprise, Judge Newton was not impressed with our setpiece on the Confederate flag or analogies to lynching, nor was there a ruling on District Attorney Tommy Floyd's later request to reassign the trial to his judicial district. There now has been a long wait—and more months added to Moore's life—for the judge to schedule the trial, which he is expected to do shortly.

And so, someday soon I will drive out of Athens to the northeast, in the opposite direction from the road that took me to Sparta or the one that took me to McDonough. Since that day in the Henry County Courthouse, I have moved to Massachusetts, so I will go back to Georgia to make this new trip. There are many good friends in Athens where I will start out, but I will drive to Thomson alone.

I HAVE BEEN alone with this book, this subject since that
September day in the courthouse when I first met Tanya Greene,
Mary Sinclair, and the others from 83 Poplar at the Moore hearing; first saw and heard Palmer Singleton and Stephen Bright;
saw and heard Tommy Floyd and Joseph Newton; saw deputy
sheriffs; saw Carzell Moore. I had seen some of the workers on
the long line assembling the intricate parts of the killing
machine that drives so relentlessly across our land. Some few
were doing their brilliant best to slip wrenches into the works to
stall it—ultimately to stop it. Others, waved on with the patriot-
ic fervor usually reserved for a war, labored at tightening the
bolts, securing the wiring.

When I drive out of Athens again into still more Georgia, I
will pass once-cotton fields on which cattle graze; at Washington
I may bypass the bypass and linger a minute or two in front of
the handsome antebellum house of friends; the house has been
in the family since long before the Civil War. Legend has it that
just across the country road, in April 1865, a company of black
soldiers, some of them Georgians, set up camp; they were in pur-
suit of Jefferson Davis just ahead of them. As it can in the South,
history almost engulfs me.

I will encounter it again further east in Thomson. There are
ghosts of the best and the worst of Georgia in that town. It was
Tom Watson's home town, he who once, late in the last century,
held out promise of a better way for Georgia's workers, both
black and white, and who, in defeat and frustration, abetted
some of the worst racist violence of this century. Thomson today
has an example, in bloom, of the newest of the New Souths: a
vastly successful nursery supplying flowering greenery for the
nation's suburbs.

There are reminders too in Thomson of a South different from
either Watson's or the newer one of blooming suburbs. Just outside
town a local man, fresh out of college, got the state to put up a historical marker to Blind Willie McTell, a great black jazz man who
lived at that corner and whom the town seemed to have forgotten.

When I get into the small crowded downtown, I'll park my car, somewhere, and climb the stairs of another Georgia courthouse. When I walk into the courtroom this time, I will see the familiar 83 Poplar Street faces; they will all be there to absorb the litany of ideas that Stephen Bright will weave into his plea to the jury to save Carzell Moore. Again, he will deliver, to use the proper nineteenth-century word, so quaint in the twentieth, an oration. With the might of commitment, of intellect, and of sheer will, Bright will try to persuade twelve citizens of McDuffie County that a person must have his life, knowing that the man sitting next to him was once so grossly in violation of another's life.

I will know the people from the office, but I will sit apart from them. I will do so because I am not one of them. I can and do share their convictions, but I do not work alongside them. All I can do is the job I undertook what seems so long ago—to tell their story.

The people of 83 Poplar are the protectors of life, lives lived in proximity to death. For a nation capable of better to allow its states to take one life as revenge for another life is to practice violence, not combat it. The death penalty is the very antithesis of civility. As the late Justice William Brennan wrote, "The state, even as it punishes, must treat its members with respect for their intrinsic worth as human beings."[1] Since Brennan's remark, the nation has coarsened, the death penalty its most rasping edge. It represents a yielding to hatred in a world too full of hatred and killing.

The people of 83 Poplar Street will not go away. As overwhelming as seems the dominance of people who disagree with them, who demand and get executions, this tiny band finally will not be beaten. Since the Furman decision a quarter century ago, with its hope of extinction of the death penalty, they have seen things get worse. History has a way of doing that. But changes for the better are not unknown. Their voices will herald that change—voices that finally will sound in Georgia's courtrooms and those of sister states across the land, in our federal courtrooms, and even in the Supreme Court in Washington. Justices Thurgood Marshall and William Brennan may be gone, but feeble as it seems, their legacy is not depleted.

Someday there will be a Juanita Jones who will snap us to attention and win over even the most reluctant to learn. The result will be the same for all murderers, not just the few now executed. According to terms either compassionate or stern, they will live a life of grave restraint in prison. For America, it will be a reprieve from vengeance and hatred.

When that day comes and I chance to drive from Athens to Sparta, the startling antique beauty of its courthouse will tell me I am in a different Georgia. I will know that the horror of a murder still beckons citizens to climb its steps in hope of witnessing American criminal law at work. There will be a defendant, a client, sitting with his lawyer; together, they will face the judgment of twelve jurors. I will know that those jurors must deal with one death—but not by inflicting a second. Life, however constrained, will be death's nearby neighbor, to whom the jurors will turn in honor of human dignity.

NOTES

1. A GEORGIA COURTHOUSE

1. Robert Frost, "The Black Cottage," in *The Complete Poems of Robert Frost* (New York: Henry Holt, 1949), 74–77.
2. For two accounts, from differing professional perspectives, see James R. Loney, *A Dream of the Tattered Man and Other Meditations: A Record of Visits to Georgia's Death Row* (Grand Rapids, MI: William B. Eerdmans Publishing Co., forthcoming 1999); Phyllis Goldfarb, "A Clinic Runs Through It," *Clinical Law Review*, vol. 1, 65 (1994).
3. We historians have been lax; no comprehensive history of the death penalty in the United States since the Civil War exists. In contrast, there are many substantial works by sociologists and innumerable excellent law review articles.

2. THE GRAND DRAGON

1. W. Fitzhugh Brundage, *Lynching in the New South: Georgia and Virginia, 1880–1930* (Urbana: University of Illinois Press, 1993).

2. *Callins* v. *Collins*, 510 US 1141, 1145 (1994) (Blackmun dissenting).
3. Obituary of Fred Speaker, *New York Times*, Sept. 16, 1996, B9.
4. "Will You Act as Individual, or Go with Crowd?" *Atlanta Constitution*, Jan. 13, 1993, C4.
5. *State of Georgia* v. *Carzell Moore*, Case No. 77CR-8676, transcript of motions proceedings, 47, (Superior Court of Monroe Co., GA, Sept. 28, 1995).
6. Ibid., 87.
7. Ibid., 88.
8. Ibid., 90.
9. Ibid., 105–06.
10. Ibid., 129. See Michael L. Radelet and Glenn L. Pierce, "Choosing Those Who Will Die: Race and the Death Penalty in Florida," 43 *Florida Law Rev.* 1 (1991). With Hugo Adam Bedau, Radelet published the "Bedau and Radelet Study," which documented the cases of 350 persons wrongfully convicted of capital or potentially capital crimes in this century. See Hugo Adam Bedau and Michael L. Radelet, "Miscarriages of Justice in Potentially Capital Cases," 40 *Stanford Law Rev.* 21 (1987). This was subsequently updated and published in Michael L. Radelet et al., *In Spite of Innocence: Erroneous Convictions in Capital Cases* (Boston: Northeastern University Press, 1992). See also Michael L. Radelet et al., "Prisoners Released from Death Rows Since 1970 Because of Doubts About Their Guilt," 13TM *Cooley Law Rev.* 907 (1996). The Supreme Court case holding that race cannot be the sole criterion for dismissing a potential juror was *Batson* v. *Kentucky*, 476 US 79 (1986). *Batson* was extended to prevent criminal defendants from dismissing jurors because of race. See *Georgia* v. *McCollum*, 505 US 42 (1992).
11. *Moore* transcript, 151.
12. Ibid., 175 ("So we're all racists" was heard but did not appear in the transcript).
13. Ibid., 189.
14. Ibid., 189–91. See Helen Prejean, *Dead Man Walking: An Eyewitness Account of the Death Penalty in the United States* (New York: Random House, 1993), and the film *Dead Man Walking* (New York: PolyGram Video, 1996).
15. *Moore* transcript, 192.

16. Ibid., 193.
17. Ibid., 194.
18. Ibid., 199–202.
19. Ibid., 203–04.
20. Ibid., 204.
21. Ibid., 205–06.
22. Ibid., 208, 211.
23. Ibid., 211–12.
24. Ibid., 214–15.

3. ATHENS

1. *Callins* v. *Collins*, 510 US 1141, 1145 (1994), (Blackmun dissenting).
2. Ibid., 1141–43; Robin Toone, in conversation with the author, Nov. 13, 1995.
3. James W. Marquart and Jonathan R. Sorenson, "A National Study of the *Furman*-Commuted Inmates: Assessing the Threat to Society from Capital Offenders," 23 *Loyola Law Rev.* 5 (1989); Radelet and Pierce, "Choosing Those Who Will Die," in Hugo Adam Bedau, ed., *The Death Penalty in America*, 3rd ed. (New York: Oxford University Press, 1982), 176.
4. Rusk quoted in Louis P. Masur, *Rites of Execution: Capital Punishment and the Transformation of American Culture, 1776–1865* (New York: Oxford University Press, 1989), 65.
5. See ibid., 160.
6. Douglas Martin, "Amazing! Incredible! Siamese Sideshow," *New York Times*, June 1, 1966.
7. William J. Bowers, *Legal Homicide: Death as Punishment in America, 1864–1982* (Boston: Northeastern University Press, 1984), 9; Victoria Schneider and John Ortiz Smykla, "A Summary Analysis of Executions in the United States, 1608–1987: The Espy File," in Robert M. Bohm, ed., *The Death Penalty in America: Current Research* (Highland Heights, KY: Academy of Criminal Justice Sciences, Northern Kentucky University, 1991), 6–7; Brundage, *Lynching in the New South*, 14; Stewart E. Tolnay and E. M. Beck, *A Festival of Violence: An Analysis of Southern Lynchings, 1882–1930* (Urbana: University of Illinois Press, 1995), 261.

8. Schneider and Smykla, "Summary Analysis," 6; Hugo Adam Bedau, *Death Is Different: Studies in the Morality, Law, and Politics of Capital Punishment* (Boston: Northeastern University Press, 1987), 148.
9. The case was *Furman* v. *Georgia*, 408 US 238 (1972).
10. *Furman*, 408 US 238, 290, 305.
11. Ibid., 309.
12. Ibid., 312.
13. Ibid., 406, 414.
14. Ibid., 464–65.
15. Ibid., 465.
16. Bill Rankin, "Fairness of the Death Penalty Is Still on Trial, Some Say It's a Matter of Race, Luck," *Atlanta Journal-Constitution*, June 29, 1997, A13.
17. *Gregg* v. *Georgia*, 428 US 153 (1976); Rhonda Cook, "Georgia Cases Have Set Legal Precedent," *Atlanta Journal-Constitution*, June 2, 1996, C4; Ken Foskett, "Evidence of Inmate's Slaying Barred in Death Penalty Trial," *Atlanta Constitution*, Sept. 6, 1990, J2.
18. *Gregg*, 428 US 153, 229–31.
19. Ibid., 232.
20. Robert Bork, Brief for the United States, at 46 *Greg* v. *Georgia*, 428 US 153 (1976) (No. 74-6257).
21. Donald G. Matthews, "The Southern Rite of Human Sacrifice," unpublished manuscript, 1–49, 25, 18.
22. John Hubbard, in conversation with the author, Nov. 15, 1997.

4. 83 POPLAR STREET

1. Tanya Greene, in conversation with the author, Nov. 17, 1997. Unless otherwise cited, all quotations in this chapter are from interviews, at different times, with the person speaking.
2. Mary Sinclair, in conversation with the author.
3. *McMillian* v. *State*, 570 S2d 1285 (Ala Crim App 1990).
4. "Remarks of Stephen B. Bright Accepting the American Bar Association's Thurgood Marshall Award," Toronto, Aug. 1, 1998.
5. The *Gilmore* case was the subject of Normal Mailer's, *The Executioner's Song* (Boston: Little, Brown, 1979).
6. This discussion of John Spenkelink is drawn from David von

Drehle, *Among the Lowest of the Dead: The Culture of Death Row* (New York: Times Books, 1995), 3–116.

7. Ibid., 103.
8. Ibid., 83–84.

5. BIRMINGHAM, ALABAMA

1. Mary Sinclair, in conversation with the author, May 21, 1996.
2. *State of Alabama v. Kenneth Eugene Smith*, cc 89-1149, trial transcript (Circuit Court of Jefferson Co. on change of venue from Colbert Co.) 1230.
3. Ibid., 762.
4. Ibid., 762, 769, 764.
5. Death Penalty Information Center, Washington, D.C., Website, http://www.essential.org/dpic
6. *Smith* transcript, 1189–91.
7. George Kendall, in conversation with the author, Oct., 30, 1997.
8. *Harris* v. *Alabama*, 513 US 504, 519 (1995), (Stevens dissenting).
9. Ibid., 526.
10. Lloyd Harper, Jr., author's telephone interview, Aug. 27, 1998.

6. DEATH IN COLUMBUS

1. The account of the deaths of Cleopholus Land and T. Z. Cotton (T.Z. McElhaney) is taken from Bill Winn, "Incident at Wynn's Hill," *Columbus Sunday Ledger* and *Columbus Ledger-Enquirer*, Jan. 25–31, 1987. The lengthy article series, heavily illustrated with contemporary photographs, contains quotations from several newspapers, including the *Columbus Ledger-Enquirer*. All quotations are from the Winn articles.
2. Bill Winn, in conversation with the author, Dec. 1, 1995.
3. Bill Winn, "Brewer's Life, Death Helped Shape Our History," *Columbus Sunday Ledger*, April 24, May 1, and May 8, 1988.
4. *State of Georgia* v. *William Anthony Brooks*, Indictment 38888, trial transcript 487 (Superior Court of Muscogee Co., Nov. 15–18, 1977).
5. Ibid., 489–90.
6. Ibid., 768.
7. Ibid., 824.

8. Ibid., 842–43.
9. Ibid., 850.
10. Ibid., 859–60.
11. Ibid., 861.
12. Ibid., 862–63.
13. Ibid., 864.
14. Ibid., 865–66.
15. Ibid., 868–69.
16. Ibid., 869–72.
17. Ibid., 873.
18. Ibid., 876–77.
19. Ibid., 890.
20. Gwendolyn Brooks, in conversation with the author, May 3, 1997.

7. THE UNDERGROUND RAILROAD

1. Obituary of Harriet Pratt Morris, *New York Times*, March 26, 1997.
2. Harriet Pratt Morris, telephone conversation with the author, April 14, 1996.
3. Ken Driggs, "A Current of Electricity Sufficient in Intensity to Cause Immediate Death: A Pre-*Furman* History of Florida's Electric Chair," 22 *Stetson Law Rev.* 1169 n.5 (1993).
4. George Kendall, telephone conversation with the author, Aug. 5, 1996.
5. Ibid.
6. George Kendall, in conversation with the author, Oct. 30, 1997.
7. Ibid.
8. Ibid.
9. Ibid.

8. WILLIAM BROOKS

1. William A. Brooks, telephone conversation with the author, Nov. 17, 1997.
2. *State of Georgia* v. *William Anthony Brooks*, Case No. 90CC-364, trial transcript, 2893–94 (Superior Court of Morgan Co., Jan. 7–23, 1991).
3. Ibid., 2930.

4. Ibid., 2932.
5. Ibid., 2932–33.
6. Ibid., 2933.
7. George Kendall, taped interview with the author, Sept. 26, 1996.
8. Ibid.
9. Ibid.
10. Ibid.
11. *Brooks* v. *Francis*, 716 F2d 780, 789 (11th Cir 1983).
12. George Kendall, taped interview with the author, Sept. 26, 1996.
13. *Brooks* v. *Kemp*, 762 F2d 1383, 1389 (11th Cir 1985).
14. George Kendall, taped interview with the author, Sept. 26, 1996.
15. *McCleskey* v. *Kemp*, 481 US 279 (1987); the Baldus study, which was presented to the Supreme Court, is published in David C. Baldus et al., "Monitoring and Evaluating Contemporary Death Sentencing Systems: Lessons from Georgia," 18 *U.C. Davis Law Rev.* 1375 (1985). And more recently in David C. Baldus et al., *Equal Justice and the Death Penalty: A Legal and Empirical Analysis* (Boston: Northeastern University Press, 1990).
16. *McCleskey* v. *Kemp*, 481 US, 279, 314–15.
17. Ibid, 339.
18. George Kendall, taped interview with the author, Sept. 26, 1996.
19. Ruth Friedman, telephone conversation with the author, July 18, 1997.
20. Ibid.
21. William Anthony Brooks, in conversation with the author, Nov. 17, 1992.

9. PHILLIPS STATE PRISON

1. Interview with Sadie Meazel (Amadeo's sister), undated notes taken by a Southern Center for Human Rights (SCHR, Atlanta, Georgia) investigator.
2. Ibid.
3. All quoted statements in this chapter are by Tony B. Amadeo in conversation with the author, Phillips State Prison, Jan. 18, 1997.
4. *State of Georgia* v. *Tony B. Amadeo*, Trial Case No. 8429, trial transcript 225 (Superior Court of Putnam Co., Nov. 28, 1977).
5. Testimony of E. R. Lambert, *Amadeo* v. *Kemp*, Civ. A. No. 84-76-

1-MAC, hearing transcript (M.D. Ga., Nov. 15, 1985) (included as Appendix to Petitioner's brief to U.S. Supreme Court, *Amadeo* v. *Zant*, 486 US 214, 235 (1988), (cited hereafter as Appendix).

6. The account that follows is taken from a fourteen-page handwritten document by Tony B. Amadeo, Amadeo Files, SCHR.

7. Testimony of Christopher Coates before Judge Wilbur D. Owens, Jr., *Bailey* v. *Vining*, Civ. A. No. 76-199-MAC (M.D. Ga., Aug. 15–17, 1978) (Evidentiary Hearing at 118–19; Order of Aug. 17, 1978, at 7); quoted in Appendix, 77–78.

8. Testimony of Christopher Coates, *Amadeo* v. *Kemp*, quoted in Appendix, 47.

9. Stephen B. Bright, quoted in *Fulton County Daily Report*, June 2, 1988.

10. See testimony of C. Nelson Jernigan, *Amadeo* v. *Kemp*, quoted in Appendix, 57.

11. Order and Memorandum Decision of Judge Owens, *Bailey* v. *Vining*, quoted in Appendix, 71.

12. Telephone interview with William Warner, April 14, 1996.

13. *Fulton County Daily Report*, Oct. 22, 1990.

14. Mary Sinclair, in conversation with the author.

15. Ruth Friedman, telephone interview with the author, July 18, 1997.

16. *Fulton County Daily Report*, Oct. 22, 1990.

17. Mark Curriden, "Fees for Pleas Called Improper," *ABA Journal* (May 1993), 28.

18. Ibid.

10. MORGAN COUNTY COURTHOUSE

1. Notes of interview with Gloria Crew, Oct. 19, 1996.

2. Rhonda Mealor, taped interview with the author, Nov. 15, 1997.

3. Gary Parker, in telephone interview with the author, Aug. 24, 1998.

4. Crew interview.

5. Voir dire of John Hubbard, *State of Georgia* v. *William Anthony Brooks*, Case No. 90CC-364, trial transcript (Superior Court of Morgan Co., Jan 7–23, 1991), Jan. 11. Voir dire of Juanita Jones, Jan., 8, ibid., 414–32.

6. Crew interview.

7. Parker interview.
8. Notes of interviewers and lawyers preparing for voir dire, SCHR.
9. Crew interview.
10. *Brooks* (1991) transcript, 2701.
11. John Hubbard, taped interview with the author, Nov. 15, 1997; Mealor interview.
12. *Brooks* (1991) transcript, 2724.
13. Parker interview.
14. William Brooks, interview with the author, Autry State Prison, Sept. 18, 1998.
15. *Brooks* (1991) transcript, 2734–35.
16. Ibid., 2737.

11. "JUST PLAIN MEAN"

1. Notes of interview with Gloria Crew, Oct. 19, 1996.
2. *State of Georgia* v. *William Anthony Brooks*, Case No. 90CC-364, trial transcript, 2994–95 (Superior Court of Morgan Co., Jan. 7–23, 1991).
3. Gary Parker, telephone interview with the author, Aug. 24, 1998.
4. Rhonda Mealor, taped interview with the author, Nov. 15, 1997.
5. *Brooks* (1991) transcript, 3340.
6. Ibid., 3354.
7. Ibid., 3355, 3351.
8. Ibid., 3352.
9. Ibid., 3378.
10. Ibid.
11. Ibid.
12. Ibid., 3379.
13. Ibid., 3380.
14. Ibid., 3382.
15. Ibid.
16. Ibid., 3383–84.
17. Ibid., 3390, 3391.
18. Ibid., 2995, 3409.
19. Ibid., 3397
20. Ibid., 3422.
21. Ibid., 3422.
22. Ibid., 3431.

23. Ibid., 3441.
24. Crew interview.
25. Mealor interview.
26. Ibid.
27. Larry Johnson, taped interview with the author, Nov. 15, 1997.
28. Ibid.
29. Ibid.
30. Parker interview.
31. Notes of interviewers and lawyers preparing for voir dire, SCHR.
32. Mealor interview.
33. *Brooks* (1991) transcript, 3464.
34. Parker interview.
35. Kimball Perry, *Columbus Ledger-Enquirer*, Jan. 24, 1991.
36. Crew interview.
37. Mealor interview.
38. Johnson interview.
39. Ruth Friedman, telephone interview with the author, July 1997.
40. Crew interview.
41. Mealor interview.
42. John Hubbard, taped interview with the author, Nov. 15, 1997.

12. JIMMY AUTRY STATE PRISON

1. William Brooks, interview with the author, Sept. 18, 1998, Autry State Prison. Unless otherwise cited, all quotations in this chapter are from the Brooks interview.

13. ACROSS GEORGIA

1. *Furman*, 408 US 238, 270.

INDEX